Feeling Queer or Queer Feelings?

Feeling Queer or Queer Feelings? presents highly innovative and contemporary ideas for counsellors, counselling and clinical psychologists and psychotherapists to consider in their work with non-heterosexual clients.

Ground-breaking ideas are presented by new thinkers in the area for issues such as:

- coming out
- transgender desire
- theoretical modalities in working with HIV
- the role of therapy in bondage and discipline, domination and submission, and sadomasochism
- the use of queer theory in therapeutic research.

Feeling Queer or Queer Feelings? will challenge present ideas about sex, gender and sexuality, and will prove to be invaluable for clinicians in this field.

Lyndsey Moon is an ESRC Research Fellow in the Department of Sociology at Warwick University. She is also a highly specialist counselling psychologist for Central and North West London Mental Health Trust.

Feeling Queer or Queer Feelings?

Radical approaches to counselling sex, sexualities and genders

Edited by Lyndsey Moon

Routledge
Taylor & Francis Group

LONDON AND NEW YORK

First published 2008 by Routledge
27 Church Road, Hove, East Sussex BN3 2FA

Simultaneously published in the USA and Canada
by Routledge
270 Madison Avenue, New York NY 10016

Routledge is an imprint of the Taylor & Francis Group, an Informa business

© 2008 selection and editorial matter, Lyndsey Moon; individual chapters,
the contributors

Typeset in Times by Garfield Morgan, Swansea, West Glamorgan
Printed and bound in Great Britain by TJ International Limited, Padstow,
Cornwall
Paperback cover design by Lisa Dynan

This publication has been produced with paper manufactured to strict
environmental standards and with pulp derived from sustainable forests.

British Library Cataloguing in Publication Data
A catalogue record for this book is available from the British Library

Library of Congress Cataloging-in-Publication Data
Feeling queer or queer feelings? : radical approaches to counselling sex,
sexualities and genders / edited by Lyndsey Moon.
        p. ; cm.
   Includes bibliographical references.
   ISBN-13: 978-0-415-38520-6 (hbk)
   ISBN-13: 978-0-415-38521-3 (pbk)
   1. Homosexuality. 2. Sex. 3. Gender identity disorders. I. Moon, Lyndsey,
1959–
   [DNLM: 1. Homosexuality–psychology. 2. Sex Counseling–methods.
3. Sexual and Gender Disorders–psychology. 4. Sexuality–psychology.
WM 611 F295 2008]
   RC451.4.G39F44 2008
   616.85'83–dc22

                                                            2007015934

ISBN: 978–0–415–38520–6 (hbk)
ISBN: 978–0–415–38521–3 (pbk)

To my Mum and Dad, and in memory
of my brother Guy. Thank you.

Contents

List of contributors

Meg Barker is a senior lecturer at London South Bank University. She teaches the psychology of sex and gender, critical psychology, counselling, and qualitative and quantitative methods. She researches sexual identities, practices and communities with a particular focus on bisexualities, non-monogamies and bondage and discipline, domination and submission, and sadomasochism (BDSM). She has published in both academic journals and popular magazines including the *Journal of Constructivist Psychology*, *The Psychologist*, and *Diva magazine*. Meg is the honorary secretary for the Lesbian and Gay Psychology Section of the British Psychological Society and co-editor of the *Lesbian & Gay Psychology Review*. She is currently training to become an existential psychotherapist specialising in sex and relationship therapy, and she is politically active in the communities she researches.

Catherine Butler works as a clinical psychologist in the field of sexual health at the Mortimer Market Centre and Archway Sexual Health Clinics, as well as a clinical tutor at the University of East London on the clinical psychology training course. She trained at the University of East London, qualifying in 2003, and completed an MSc in Systemic Therapy in 2006. She provides training in sexuality awareness on all the North Thames clinical psychology training courses and for Pink Therapy. She also provides in-house training in the North Thames NHS Trust for an accredited foundation course in systemic therapy. Catherine was previously on the Lesbian and Gay Psychology section of the British Psychological Society and is currently an active member on the HIV and Sexual Health Committee. Her research interests to date have been around personal/professional development for lesbian and gay clinical psychology trainees and working with interpreters in the field of sexual health.

Angela Byrne has worked as a clinical psychologist in the field of sexual health and HIV since 1999. She is currently working as a clinical tutor on the clinical psychology training course at the University of East

London. She is also employed by Barts and the London NHS Trust on a sexual health outreach project for people living with HIV. She has been employed as an international consultant on HIV programme development and training by various organisations including WHO, UNAIDS, UNICEF and Family Health International. She trained at the University of East London, qualifying in 1999. Prior to training as a clinical psychologist, she completed a PhD on anxiety and depression and worked as a research psychologist in the field of substance misuse. Her clinical and research interests include women's sexual health, service provision for refugees, black and minority ethnic communities, and training staff in HIV/sexual health services.

Camelia Gupta is a mental health worker, independent researcher and journalist. She worked for several years in a voluntary capacity for Threshold Women's Mental Health Initiative providing support and listening to a broad range of clients. A member of several working groups concerning lesbian, gay, bisexual and transgender mental health, she has written on sexuality, bondage and discipline, domination and submission, and sadomasochism (BDSM), safe space and mental health for a number of publications. She also writes about visual culture, contemporary art and performance and has an MA in Visual Cultures from Goldsmiths College, University of London.

Peter Hegarty is a senior lecturer at the University of Surrey with interests in social psychology and the history of psychology. His work in both fields focuses on LGBT issues and on 'normativity' – the ways that certain groups and practices become privileged as simply human, while others must argue brave, endless nature–nurture battles to become recognised as such. He was on the board of the Center for Lesbian and Gay Studies in New York and the Lesbian and Gay Psychology section of the British Psychological Society. He taught courses on lesbian, gay, bisexual and transgender psychology while studying at Stanford University and while visiting at Yale University and the University of Michigan.

Myra J. Hird is a professor of sociology and Queen's National Scholar at Queen's University in Canada. She has written two monographs as well as numerous articles on topics including violence and gender, and intersex, trans and the ontology of sexual difference. Her most recent work focuses on science studies, specifically microbiology and theories of social relating.

Ian Hodges is a senior lecturer in psychology at the University of Westminster. His research interests include psychology, power and social regulation, psychotherapeutic discourse, sexual prejudice, sexual identity and social psychological aspects of HIV. He teaches critical psychology, social psychology, lesbian and gay psychology and qualitative methods. He is currently training at the Institute of Group Analysis.

Alessandra Iantaffi is an active researcher and lecturer in the fields of diversity, inclusion, identities and research theories and methodologies. Since moving to the UK, she took her PhD at the University of Reading. It focused on the experiences of disabled women students in higher education, and her thesis was awarded the British Educational Research Association Award as best dissertation in educational research for 1999. She has taught several aspects of disability studies, equity in education, women's studies, inclusion, sexuality and young people and research methodology, as well as being involved in various research projects. Alessandra has used both quantitative and qualitative methodologies during the course of her research and is particularly committed to the use of personal construct psychology (PCP) and social constructionism as theoretical and methodological frameworks. She is about to qualify as a systemic family psychotherapist and is currently pursuing a portfolio of activities on a part-time basis while raising her daughter.

Darren Langdridge is a lecturer in social psychology at the Open University and an existential psychotherapist. His work is principally concerned with the application of the hermeneutic phenomenology of Paul Ricoeur to understand the construction of 'new' sexual identities and the dynamic making of selves within different personal and social contexts. He is the author of *Introduction to Research Methods and Data Analysis in Psychology* and *Phenomenological Psychology: Theory, Research and Method* (both Pearson Education) as well as numerous papers on sexualities, the construction of 'the family' and existential psychotherapy.

Lyndsey Moon is an ESRC Research Fellow in the Department of Sociology at Warwick University. She is also a highly specialist counselling psychologist for Central and North West London Mental Health Trust. Her research interests include queer theory, symbolic interaction, and the interaction of sexualities and emotion. She has worked on a number of committees within the British Psychological Society. She also works privately as a chartered counselling psychologist in North West London.

Tam Sanger has a PhD in *Transpeople's Intimate Partnerships and the Cultural Construction of Gender and Sexuality*. Her research interests include queer theory, governmentality, medicalisation, asexuality, transgender and polyamoury. She works as a teaching assistant at Queen's University, Belfast.

Acknowledgements

This book is a first in addressing the impact and meaning of queer theory in counselling, clinical psychology and psychotherapy. It is also a first in drawing together the disciplines of psychology and sociology within this field and it highlights the growing need for counsellors and psychotherapists to develop a psychosocial project in relation to their work with all clients but specifically in relation to gender, sex, sexuality and emotion.

All those who have contributed to this book are given special thanks for contributing their time, energy and ideas. I must also say thank you to Steve Palmer who gave me the encouragement to approach Routledge with the idea in the first place, to Joanne Forshaw and Claire Lipscomb at Routledge for their editorial skills and to all those who have helped in the production of this book.

Thanks also to Diane Richardson who offered plenty of ideas while I studied at Newcastle University and especially to the ESRC who gave me that opportunity. Many thanks to Warwick University for offering me a Visiting Fellowship and access to their wonderful library. However, above all, a very special thank you is awarded to Ken Plummer who both inspired me and supported my ideas while I studied at Essex University. Thanks Ken.

I would like to thank my parents for all their love and support over the years and my partner Lalla, whose love and life I am privileged to share. Finally, and tragically, my brother died before this book was finished. I would like to thank him for just being my brother who I deeply loved.

Chapter 1

Introduction

Queer(y)ing a psychosocial approach to sex, sexuality and gender in therapeutic settings

Lyndsey Moon

> Queer describes those gestures or analytical models which dramatise
> incoherencies in the allegedly stable relations between chromosomal sex,
> gender and sexual desire.
>
> Jagose (1998:3)

Despite the growing popularity of queer theory in sociology, lesbian, gay and
bisexual studies; literary and cultural studies; and its undoubted impact on
the politics of sex, gender and sexuality; the academic and applied world of
counselling, counselling/clinical psychology and psychotherapy (referred to
as therapy from here on in) has been suspiciously silent about the matter.
And, if we were to believe counsellors, counselling and clinical psychologists
and psychotherapists, none of the clients who attend therapy has any queer
concerns either. Therapy, it has to be said, has not been queered, despite
there being much to query! And yet, because queer is an approach that
combines theoretical innovation with reactionary tendencies, especially in
relation to sex, sexuality and gender, it provides an ideal challenge to the
conventions of therapeutic endeavours. In an effort to initiate a discourse
that merges different strands of thinking in relation to therapy, I have
brought together a number of authors from psychology, counselling and
sociology who may be considered to be somewhat dissident in their opinions
towards sex, gender and sexuality when compared to conventional views held
by most therapists. However, as I see it, these authors are providing the
foundation for crucial debates that need to be developed and researched
within the realms of counselling, counselling/clinical psychology and psychotherapy as well as suggesting future directions in theory and research and for
that reason they should be applauded for their 'risky behaviour'.

The Noah's ark of therapy

From their inception, binary categories have been the centrepiece of
modernity, separating men from women, male from female, black from

white, homosexual from heterosexual, able bodies from disabled bodies. Ideologically, this form of thinking has underpinned therapeutic structures, constructing the various models into an enterprise that is remarkably consistent with binary configurations. Despite the rhetoric that suggests therapy promotes individual freedom, such freedoms are sanctioned and constrained by social discourses and regulatory practices when people present as truly 'individual' in the eyes of the therapist. This is certainly the case where issues relating to sex, gender and sexuality are presented that fall outside of the conventional social markers for these configurations. This interrogates the notion of 'freedom' for the 'individual' extensively, because the unconventional individual poses a threat to established therapeutic discourse as well as challenging the meaning of freedom within the thera-peutic space. An intersex person going to a therapist is likely to be faced with ignorance and questions while the therapist searches for the psychological condition of gender identity dysphoria (GID), where gender is primarily arranged as two diametrically opposed bodies, and all bodies are then com-pared against this construction. It is the therapist rather than the client who may be troubled by the shift and change of conventional to unconventional meanings, but it is the client rather than the therapist who may have to bear the consequences. As Hegarty points out (Chapter 9), it is important to realise that therapists are 'very ordinary' people 'situated within culture' and are open to the same prejudices and ignorance as lay people.

Even more troubling to therapy will be the 'queer' client, who presents and represents 'otherness', a sort of sexed, sexualised and gendered oddity whose body carries no fixed meaning in relation to sex, gender or sexuality. Instead, this client presents as multi-identity, the body carrying a plurality of meanings drawn from many different strands of identities in action. The therapist is unable to attach binary meanings to the client in the interaction and this will influence the narratives that emerge in the therapeutic working alliance as well as how these meanings interrogate therapeutic models. This book represents some of these new ways of thinking that will hopefully disrupt therapeutic ideology and provide a new therapeutic topography for practitioners and theoreticians to explore.

Queer solutions

All the chapters provide queer theoretical challenges a) to normative accounts of sex, gender and sexuality by challenging the generally held belief that these are biologically driven and 'naturally' organised and b) to the notable presence of heterosexual hegemony and how this is represented through the various therapeutic models that fail to take into account non-heterosexual discourses in relation to sex, sexuality and gender. Each chapter carries a theoretical and psychosocial perspective that with hope, readers will want to develop and research in relation to their work with clients. The overall purpose is to challenge our binary thinking, to prevent the either/or rhetoric that has been a purposeful tool of modernity, pervading most theoretical and applied social systems. These challenges are embodied within the chapters so that alongside new knowledge that may be applied to therapeutic issues via theory and/or practice this knowledge may also be extended, applied and employed to initiate new debates and disputes within therapeutic contexts e.g. training of students. Some ways of framing these debates include: a) the impact of ideology on the shaping of therapeutic models and how this reflects the much wider heterosexualised structural and social ordering of society; b) the meaning and negotiation of emotion and how this may be used as a system of regulation within therapeutic ideology and practice; c) how meanings for gender are imposed onto and into the body and how this remains configured through heterosexuality; d) meanings of sex, sexuality and gender for therapists when presented by clients who are assigned to 'non-normative' categories; e) HIV and how meanings for this are integrated socially as well as therapeutically for both client and therapist; f) the meanings of sex and sex roles when we interact within adult, consensual, sexual relationships; g) the way research may employ queer theory and what this means for research design and interpretation.

Each chapter aims to address the above debates through theoretical perspectives and complexities in relation to the cultural, encounter and personal narratives or scripts of the therapist and the client, and to show how these are negotiated within the therapeutic encounter. The chapters include theoretical perspectives in relation to power within the therapeutic encounter, coming out of heterosexuality, the negotiation of emotion within therapy, theory and applied work in relation to intersexuality, the meanings for transgender sexuality, working with HIV and the sexual negotiation of bondage and discipline, domination and submission, and sadomasochism (BDSM) within sexualised interactions.

In Chapter Two, Ian Hodges clearly sets out what queer theory is, how it emerged and the implications for power and practice in the therapeutic setting. Ian raises a number of interesting questions for the reader to consider. Should we resist identity labels? How does Social Constructionism deal with the illusion of therapeutic discourse as fluid and interchangeable? Is queer theory really helpful for clients in therapeutic settings? What of clients who can only function with an 'identity' and for whom a major achievement may be to announce to one other person 'I am gay'. Central to all this is Ian's work on 'power' (understood as 'the discursive production of truth') that highlights the dilemmas operating in the therapeutic space. Ian uses the works of Foucault and Judith Butler to highlight how power 'gets inside our bodies, our "hearts" and our heads' through the use of discourse. In many ways this chapter links to the later chapter by Hegarty (Chapter Nine) who presents the experiments of Zimbardo and Milgram, because it shows how power can be used to subordinate non-heterosexualities and may even explain why and how those who worked within the psy disciplines took such brutal steps to eradicate 'homosexuality' in the past. It would be interesting to deconstruct the meanings of Milgram's experiment when applied to the past history of sexuality where scientists giving electric shocks to homosexuals were doing so 'in the name of science' and ultimately the removal of homosexuality.

In Chapter Three, Darren Langdridge explores contemporary meanings of identity models. For Darren, traditional lesbian and gay identity models render them as fixed, linear examples of modernity's quest for order and rationality. Although identity provides meaning, it can also be used to limit the endless possibilities of identity if reduced to a psychological dichotomy. Rather than earning identity bit by bit through developmental stages, Darren suggests that we should always be constructing and reconstructing identity so that, in effect, it is made useless as a binary product. At a cultural level, identity models have acted as instructional guides, telling us how we should arrange everyday social and sexual life into recognisable categories. Darren asks us to break with this idea. Introducing his own work, Darren introduces the reader to 'a radical hermeneutics of suspicion' where it is possible to work with the client beyond the apparent and challenge the client's perspective on the world by encouraging them to challenge the existing order of things. Darren provides an example of his work with a client that shows how binary positions in relation to sex, gender and sexuality may be shifted by searching out alternative examples from a range of culturally available discourses and re-positioning the self in light of these new discoveries.

In Chapter Four, I focus on the role of emotion and the way emotions, as cultural representations, are assigned onto and into the body of lesbian and gay clients by heterosexual, lesbian and gay male therapists. In this chapter, rather than emotions being understood as a *natural* product of the body, they are considered to be a socially organised set of meanings that act as a *regulatory system*, producing and reproducing binarisms that act to structure subordinate (to heterosexuality) sexualities.

Myra Hird in Chapter Five, focuses on the role of intersex, and Myra uses Freudian theory to show how conventional meanings of sexuality and gender may be disrupted through a re-reading of Freud's work. She asks us to consider how the origin of identification and desire lies in 'bisexuality' and that the process of identification relies upon 'reality through deprivations' that enact the individual's gender recognition. Masculinity and femininity as 'identity' are a form of compromise, reached through 'denial of the other', so there is always resistance to identity. Challenging the limited dichotomy of gender, she pursues the notion that far from the individual being unhappy with a given morphology, instead it is worth considering the role of doctors and therapists who impose this belief onto their subjects when in fact, it is the doctors and therapists themselves who find the body in need of surgical (usually) regulation. Myra takes up this challenge, introduces Freud's theory as a way out of the dilemma, and asks therapists to reconsider their own understanding of the intersexed body prior to working with clients. Using studies that are often cited as arguments for an 'essential' gender, where the reassigned gender for a child is later rejected once that child is old enough to make a choice (thus suggesting that there is a 'real' gender the individual wants to be according to medical interpretations), Hird suggests the selection of this alternative gender is also based on choice so that configuring an alternative gender does not necessarily mean the individual has a 'natural' gender after all.

Tam Sanger in Chapter Six, focuses on the experience of those who define as trans and the problem of assuming a binary identity fits all approach from those within the medical industry. She traces the history of trans people, questions the increasing desire to categorise and pathologise despite the instability of gender and sexuality, and suggests that practitioners think in a much broader way about their work with trans people and how it impacts on family and partners. Tam presents a series of interesting and challenging case studies that will surely provide those who are training students with a series of challenges to standard, carefully constructed, case examples.

Chapter Seven is by Catherine Butler and Angela Byrne who work as clinical psychologists in HIV and sexual health services. They take from their work with clients to suggest a queer reading of what is considered as 'normal', 'healthy' and 'desirable' behaviour. Using extensive case studies, they illustrate how therapists need to shift their ideas in order that they may work more effectively with all client groups. With this in mind they quote from their own research that shows therapists need more input in relation to sex, sexuality and gender, and they provide an outline of what training needs are required if therapists are to work effectively as well as ethically with various client populations.

Meg Barker, Alessandra Iantaffi and Camel Gupta, in Chapter Eight, focus on what seems to be taken as a form of the body in sexual theatre, where social actors may dress up, rehearse sexual scripts and endure pleasure through pain in a consensual, adult manner. They write in relation to bondage and discipline, domination and submission, and sadomasochism (BDSM) and the role of therapy and therapists when challenged by these queer sexualities. They advise of the current legal status of BDSM, why BDSM may be perceived as threatening and explore the extent to which BDSM can be constructed as a queer sexuality that challenges heteronormativity.

Finally, in Chapter Nine, Peter Hegarty presents a chapter that considers queer methodologies. Peter draws from experimental science, exploring the historical and methodological issues posed by quantitative approaches within the social sciences. However, rather than disavow the role of quantitative approaches, Peter uses these studies to present alternative ways of using their procedures and outcomes. This is particularly relevant to the works of Milgram and Zimbardo. He analyses how results are (and could be) interpreted and estimates their impact for both researchers and researched when assigned to a heteronormative framework. Peter provides evidence suggesting that before conducting research, the language, position and differences of those conducting the research in comparison to those being researched needs to be interrogated.

The overwhelming message of the book is really aimed at therapists who, it must be concluded, need to integrate a thoroughly psychosocial perspective into their approaches. Lingering in the time worn archetypes, therapists seem afraid of really challenging traditional discourses established when the world had far different ideas about sex, sexuality and gender. Each chapter provides a substantive area that asks readers for a queer perspective whereby the old rhetoric of either/or is disregarded (temporarily if not permanently), and the reader is asked to sit with the discomfort of change and new ideas. Admitting to this discomfort, to the fear of letting go of a familiar rhetoric, of stepping outside the safe boundary of sex, sexuality and gender will allow for a period of transition and a queer creativity. This project is not intended to be separatist but instead asks for a much larger social project that means radicalising therapy and providing a complete textual analysis of its very foundation that will propel it into the twenty-first century.

One final point. I have tried to let the voice of the different authors be heard throughout the chapters. Although I have edited the work, I would hope that I have not imposed myself into the chapters written by other authors. This is intentional because it is important that the plurality of ideas and identities are allowed to surface, adding to the uniqueness of queer narratives that are necessary to bring about a radicalising of therapeutic ideologies.

Reference

Jagose, A. (1998) *Queer Theory*. Victoria: Melbourne University Press.

Chapter 2

Queer dilemmas

The problem of power in psychotherapeutic and counselling practice

Ian Hodges

> A critique is not a matter of saying that things are not right as they are. It is a matter of pointing out on what kinds of assumptions, what kinds of familiar, unchallenged, unconsidered modes of thought the practices that we accept rest . . .
>
> Michel Foucault (1981/1990a:155)

Introduction

In this chapter I argue that if we take Queer Theory and activism seriously we need to be fully open to a queer critique of counselling and psychotherapeutic practices[1] and that such a critique invites us to focus upon the issue of power in therapeutic practices, especially the ways in which power operates through the (discursive) construction and reconstruction of truth(s) about the client's self. I have had a personal and professional interest in the issue of power and psychotherapy for some time and wrote my doctoral thesis on this topic (Hodges 1998). My interest originally began with the problem of the lack of voice for clients and patients in the counselling/clinical literature. However, I soon came to see that ultimately what was at stake was psychotherapeutic power itself. Not power defined as a personal characteristic (that is, something individuals have or have not, something we can give or take away) and not power as a problem of professional ethics (that is, as something to be wielded responsibly) – though these are both important formulations. Rather through my academic engagement with Queer Theory and my personal experience of queer activism I came to understand power in Foucauldian terms as the discursive production of truth (in this case truth about oneself). Put another way, here I conceive of power as operating through the shaping effects of therapeutic talk, that is, the ways in which therapeutic discourse shapes and reshapes the discourses that clients bring to counselling and therapy, which in turn (re)constitutes their self-understanding. Here I argue that so far, even with more radical constructionist/narrative approaches, practitioners have to a great extent avoided the issue of power. Following a brief exploration of the nature of Queer Theory, I outline how Michel Foucault and Judith Butler's work can be applied to therapeutic practices. I then discuss some shortfalls with radical approaches and finally I identify subsequent dilemmas for counselling and psychotherapeutic practice with queer clients.

What is Queer Theory? Dismantling the closet

Queer Theory is fundamentally about power, politics and activism. In particular, it focuses on the ways in which our most private understandings of who we are, who we desire, who and how we love, of acceptance and rejection, sameness and difference, are shaped, moulded and regulated by relations of language, power and authority. In short, Queer Theory focuses upon the ways in which power gets inside our bodies, our 'hearts' and our heads. It is above all oppositional – opposing all forms of oppression including the ways that seemingly liberatory categories, especially 'lesbian', 'gay', 'bisexual' and 'trans', may themselves become tied to (oppressive) regulatory regimes and practices.

To understand Queer Theory it is useful to begin by asking where did Queer Theory and activism come from? Queer Theory has a complex and multi-layered relation to queer politics and activism.[2] The term Queer itself was deployed in order to transcend boundaries and categories of gender, class and race, thus Queer activism took its name from the reclamation of a term of abuse – queer – which was adopted by many as a new label to replace established sexual, gender and racial/ethnic categories. It is also significant that the queer movement emerged from a highly separatist social and political context. Lesbians and gay men did not necessarily share the same concerns, needs and priorities. Lesbian culture and politics separated from the gay movement during the 1970s, finding feminism more useful for political struggle there were also divisions within the lesbian movement, most notably between socialists and radical feminists. Gay politics focused on male-centred issues, for example, AIDS services, homophobia and gross indecency, while lesbian politics focused on, for example, gender, reproduction and heteropatriarchy. Emerging from this context, Queer activism was militantly anti-separatist and emphasised provocation and transgression. Its position was profoundly anti-gender, anti-feminist, anti-'gay' and anti-'lesbian'. That is, for Queer activists, categories of gender, sexuality and race/ethnicity were not merely limiting but profoundly and dangerously (sometimes lethally) oppressive. Even feminism was rejected as too separatist, divisive and overly grounded in existing gender relations.

Queer activism then, was very much about externalising existing anger and frustration at homophobia and heteropatriarchy, aiming to channel these emotions towards personal and political resistance. The strident anger of the movement is well illustrated by the 'gays bash back' banners at pride marches during the early 1990s and the circulation of the anonymous publication in 1990 of *I hate straights*:

> Being queer means leading a different sort of life. It's not about the mainstream, profit margins, patriotism, patriarchy or being assimilated. It's not about executive directors, privilege and elitism. It's about being on the margins, defining ourselves . . . when a lot of lesbian and gay men wake up in the morning they feel angry and disgusted not gay.
>
> (Anonymous 1990:3)

Two powerful aspects of the movement then, were first its insistence on inclusivity especially its rejection of sexism and racism, and second, its capacity to focus, normalise and externalise the anger and frustration – especially among younger lesbians and gay men – which had previously failed to find an outlet. Above all, the Queer movement was based on resistance and insubordination. It identified problems with the lesbian/gay movement, believed assimilation was dangerous and that gay identity had become tied to dominant power structures. There was also a sense of frustration concerning the ghettoisation of lesbian and gay culture and despondency concerning the way that the existing lesbian and gay movements had failed to properly politicise the key issues of sexism, racism and homophobia.

This framework of rejection, resistance and insubordination does not straightforwardly map onto counselling and psychotherapeutic practices. However, as a starting point, we might ask whether our interventions with lesbian, gay, bisexual and transgender (LGBT) clients are to be recognised as practices of resistance or themselves practices bound up with therapeutic claims to authority which align clients with normalised modes of being. Put another way, while there have been and remain the more obviously oppressive forms of therapeutic practice, for example electro-shock and other forms of 'reparative' therapy for LGBT persons, Queer Theory brings with it a profound suspicion of any form of identity category (including those deemed liberatory) and any form of authority (which I suggest must include therapeutic authority). However, before these questions can be addressed we need to explore the ideas of two of the leading theorists of the Queer movement.

Michel Foucault and Judith Butler

At the heart of Queer Theory and activism is the work of Michel Foucault and Judith Butler.[3] For Foucault (1988, 1992; Rabinow 1994) a key means by which power has its effects is through the production of truth concerning oneself – what Foucault termed practices of *subjectification*. This refers to the plethora of contemporary practices – including counselling and psychotherapy – through which selves (and self-understanding) are assembled and reassembled. Rose (1985, 1990, 1992, 1996) more fully explored the ways in which psychological (especially therapeutic) discourses enjoin individuals to assemble *themselves* as ethical beings, reminding us that practices of the self are always more than linguistic constructions but rather emerge from a heterogeneity of discursive and non-discursive practices, architectural forms, locales and claims to authority.

In relation to sexuality and sexual identity, Foucault rejected any sense that sex was 'natural'. His work was fundamentally anti-foundationalist (he questions the taken-for-granted foundations of knowledge. These usually take the form of basic or self-evident beliefs and in psychology have historically been based on rationality and empiricism). His work was also anti-humanist (that is, he rejected the idea of a universal morality based on the unassailable 'truth' of human nature). Foucault was interested in historical discontinuities (he was influenced by Nietzsche among others) and emphasised that social conditions are never external to the emergence of knowledge. He conceived of sexuality and sexual identity as fictions mobilised to control sex and bodies and famously reminded us that the homosexual as a 'species' emerged only recently: 'Homosexuality appeared as one of the forms of sexuality when it was transposed from the practice of sodomy onto a kind of interior androgyny, a hermaphrodism of the soul' (Foucault 1980:43).

So, here our understandings of sex and sexuality (including sexual identity) are not linked to laws of biology or psychology but rather are products of culture and history and play a role in the regulation of bodies and populations. Queer Theory built on this anti-foundationalism seeking to move beyond liberatory identity politics and its related gender and sexual categories.

To make sense of Foucault's contribution – especially as it might impact on conceptions of therapeutic practice – I need to briefly explain what he meant by the term discourse and why this is so important. The most straightforward starting definition is that discourse refers to language-in-use, but language-in-use which is always already *situated*: historically, culturally, geographically, institutionally and above all in relation to power. In a more complex sense, discourse and discursive practices (like counselling and therapy) operate through setting out positions from which individuals may speak (for example, doctor and patient, therapist and client). They link to institutions (for example, the NHS) and they construct and enable conversations about particular objects while engendering silence about others. The term discourse then, refers to the articulation of language with certain practices and techniques, institutional forms and relations of power. Fundamentally it refers to the relations between truth (knowledge), power and identity (self).

What makes Foucault's work so central to Queer Theory is that he offered a developed theory of both power and resistance, not only in relation to sexuality but also in relation to a range of other key institutions and practices, for example, the penal system, psychiatry and medicine. Foucault sidelines models of power which emphasise domination and repression and suggests that rather than saying 'no', power in contemporary western societies is a much more positive force, operating via the often subtle and routine shaping of thought and conduct. However, these shaping forces are always open to resistance. In this way, Foucault suggested that instead of analysing power as something that crushes subjectivity we should undertake what he called an ascending analysis, starting from the smallest, seemingly routine everyday practices and procedures that are commonplace in our contemporary culture. These practices he called micro-capillaries of power, and only once the hard work of mapping these practices and techniques has been completed, can we begin to link them with broader forms of regulatory regimes such as capitalism and what Foucault termed biopower or biopolitics[4] (Foucault 1990b, 1991). Thus, using this model, counselling and therapy become an important means through which individuals are not simply regulated through therapeutic discourse but where clients' subjectivities are shaped – via the process of subjectification – through moulding the ways in which clients choose to practice their freedom.

While Foucault, especially in volume one of the *History of Sexuality*, provided a significant theoretical element of the Queer movement, it was the work of Judith Butler which offered a powerful model of resistance through her notion of the discursive, performative nature of gender and identity and the practice of what she termed 'gender insubordination'. Butler's best-known work and the text which arguably had the greatest impact on queer activists and theorists is her 1991 book *Gender Trouble* (Butler 1991). Using Foucault's methods, Butler convincingly argued that mimesis is at the heart of gender (and sexuality):

> . . . gender is a kind of imitation for which there is no original; in fact, it is a kind of imitation that produces the very notion of the original as an effect and consequence of the imitation itself.
>
> (Butler 1991:21)

In other words the taken-for-granted – seemingly real, biological – nature of gender and sexuality is a product of social performance, gender identities are practiced, stylised, 'performed'. Butler also employed the metaphor of drag to illustrate the performative nature of gender. Remember though that here gender is not a simple performance but the complex discursive operation of identity; gender is above all a product of repetition and stylisation. Butler argues that homosexuality is often considered an imitation of heterosexuality and therefore somehow secondary to it (recall the 'pretend families' of Clause 28[5]), however for her, in fact, all gender and identity categories are a kind of imitation. The most crucial lesson to learn about identity, she argued, is that it is always vulnerable to regulation:

> . . . identity categories tend to be instruments of regulatory regimes, whether as the normalising categories of oppressive structures or as the rallying points for a liberatory contestation of that very oppression.
>
> (Butler 1991:13–14)

Thus, a progressive (queer) politics must acknowledge and incorporate the dangers of self-identification to avoid the re-affirmation of compulsory heterosexuality. In other words, we must constantly and routinely resist gender and other identity categories through gender insubordination.

Psychotherapeutic authority

A Foucauldian framework then, offers a means of reflecting upon the psy sciences through a developed theory of the operation of power in relation to language and through which we might understand the regulatory nature of psychological (here therapeutic) discourse. Furthermore, Foucault's later work – with its emphasis upon self-regulation and self-discipline – enables a consideration of the therapeutic transformation of selves as a form of subjectification (involving truth telling) in which the ethical operation of psychotherapeutic discourse offers a way of understanding how the discourse (and concomitantly, power) gets 'inside' the individual, in this case the client (Hodges 2001, 2002, 2003). It is not that therapy and counselling (including radical techniques) are somehow wrong or even oppressive (though this cannot be ruled out) but rather that we need to properly understand their operation upon individuals and within society before we can make any proper evaluation (c.f. Rose 1998).

Moreover, Butler's notion of gender and sexuality as performance links to existing debates about the 'causes' of non-heterosexual desire, exemplified within psychology's modernist project through the naturalisation of causality, especially in relation to mind and body (via Descartes). That is causality, for example the 'causes' of being lesbian or gay tend to be situated within the biological realm – genes, hormones, neuronal pathways and so on. This suspicion of the biological marks much post Second World War theorising, especially among feminist writers. We might ask why biological explanations are so problematic here. Biological explanations – here understood as fictions, separated from their scientific claims to truth – tend to fix identity, allowing little or no room for imagining identities differently. Put another way, biological explanations allow little room for constructing and reconstructing alternative and less oppressive formations of gender and sexuality.

In the remainder of this chapter, I consider what these ideas and frameworks mean for counselling and therapeutic practice. The concepts outlined above leave us, I suggest, with two major challenges with regard to counselling and other affirmative therapies for LGBT clients. First, there is the issue of the extent to which we should problematise and/or resist identity, especially the categories lesbian, gay, bi and trans, and second, the issue of how we understand and deal with the power of therapeutic and counselling discourse and its relation to regulation and authority. Some of the concepts outlined here have led to 'alternative' models of practice which more explicitly acknowledge problems of power in therapy and claim to challenge power inequalities and (therapeutic) authority. In what follows, I briefly outline some of their merits and pitfalls. I then go on to discuss two key dilemmas that Queer Theory raises for practice with LGBT clients.

Social constructionist therapy

Since Bateson, Maturana and others in the 1970s and 1980s conceptualised the family as a cybernetic rule-governed system (Bateson 1972), there have been attempts to engage radical theory within the social sciences with psychotherapeutic practice. This has led to new frameworks/models of psychotherapy, most notably social constructionist and narrative therapy, both of which have links to family and systemic therapy. These models all variously contest notions of psychopathology and explicitly challenge power relations and hierarchies in therapeutic and counselling practice. Constructionist approaches have been especially popular as a means of practising lesbian, gay and bisexual affirmative counselling and psychotherapy. Simon and Whitfield (2000) describe their practice thus:

> We regard social constructionist therapy as offering a more coherent framework for therapeutic work with lesbians, gay men and bisexuals because it pays attention to practices of power and challenges assumptions about pathology, sexuality, gender and life choices. It strives to promote a reflexive; co-constructive working relationship in which both therapist and client(s) can deconstruct the assumptions in the stories each brings and reflect on the effects of those ideas.
>
> (Simon and Whitfield 2000:103)

One of the key elements of constructionism which situated it as radical within psychology, especially in the 1980s, was its insistence that the origin of 'mental' phenomena should be situated *between* people rather than *within* them (although within sociology George Herbert Mead had been arguing this since the 1930s). So constructionism offered a notion of the psychological where thoughts, beliefs and knowledge were products of communication rather than individual minds. Put another way, for social constructionists it was communication within and through dyads, groups and communities that led to the formation of experience, and this tenet forms the basis of constructionist approaches to therapy. Fruggeri (1992) outlining the notion of therapy as the 'social construction of change' argued that:

> The beliefs that construct these [individual] realities are not ideas in the minds of people, they are generated in communication processes. . . beliefs held by individuals construct realities and realities are maintained through social interaction, which, in turn, confirm the beliefs that are then socially originated.
>
> (Fruggeri 1992:43)

One of the foundations of constructionist therapy then, can be summarised as a resistance to psychologism – the assumption that knowledge (including self-knowledge) has its origins in minds and the psychological realm – and a focus upon the co-production of knowledge via a range of communication practices. The work of Anderson and Goolishian (1992) on the therapeutic practice of 'not knowing' is also popular with radical therapists and counsellors who find in it concrete guidelines for practice. Here therapy becomes a conversation between equals:

> Therapy is a linguistic event that takes place in what we call a therapeutic conversation. The therapeutic conversation is a mutual search and exploration through dialogue, a two-way exchange, a criss-crossing of ideas in which new meanings are continually evolving toward the dissolving of problems, and thus, the dissolving of the therapy system and hence the problem organizing, problem dis-solving system . . . The therapist is a participant observer and a participant facilitator of the therapeutic conversation.
>
> (Anderson and Goolishian 1992:27)

Thus, by adopting a constructionist perspective the therapist can hand back their power to the client. The role of the therapist in this scenario has very little to do with power, in fact in the terms outlined above the therapist appears to have washed her or his hands of power, she or he is simply a co-conversationalist, a participant-facilitator in the unfolding of the co-construction of the client's reality. While I would argue that treating the client as an expert in their own experience may well be useful, there is an obfuscation of power relations here which ultimately leads us away from a concrete understanding of the ways power in therapy actually operates. So far we have seen that if we take Queer Theory – and especially the work of

Foucault – seriously then we must acknowledge that therapy is intimately tied up with hierarchy and power.

I suggest that the most problematic consequence of the constructionist position is the illusion that (therapeutic) discourse is entirely fluid and (inter)changeable, having the quality of a resource which the individual can utilise/voice and interrupt at will. Fundamentally, this particular under-standing of discursive practice risks placing the site of analysis *solely* between individuals – given understandings and accounts are seen as socially negotiated and situated between people (c.f. Gergen 1985). Thus, discourse becomes another consumable; its fluid and shifting character enabling an attractive flexibility of meanings/uses and an equality of oppor-tunity to voice them. Gergen (1992) describes the advantages of such a conceptualisation of discourse:

> Patterns of human activity largely revolve around discourse; discourse serves as perhaps the critical medium through which relationships are carried out. And, *because discourse exists in an open market, marked by chaotic and broadly diffuse alteration* . . . then patterns of human action will also remain forever unfolding [my emphasis].
>
> (Gergen 1992:26)

It seems however, that in an attempt to theorise the indeterminacy of discourse as a space of resistance, we are in fact left with a liberal-humanist conception of discursive activity where each and every discourse is available to all, thus rendering power relations far less visible. In addition, con-structionism's (postmodern) rejection of truth has left it unable to account for *truth effects*. Instead of analysing therapeutic discourse as simply the co-construction of reality, I argue that we must attend to the ways certain fictions function in truth (where truth is bound up with material, including institutional, practices) – thus enabling an analysis of power other than as a perspectival interest. In other words, while social constructionist approaches bring much that is valuable to LGBT affirmative counselling and therapy, ultimately they fail to situate problems in the wider social, political and economic structures which are fundamentally bound up with the discourses (of self-understanding) that clients bring to the therapeutic exchange and the therapeutic discourses that counsellors use in their interventions.

Fruggeri (1992), laying out the fundamentals for a constructionist therapy, asks:

> What makes a conversation that particular type of conversation that changes all the other conversations? What makes a narrative a special kind of narrative that generates new narratives? My opinion is that

therapists should answer these questions in the name of a non-control-oriented constructionist thinking.

(Fruggeri 1992:49–50)

I would answer these questions by saying power – psychotherapeutic power reconceptualised as regulatory practices of the self (c.f. Miller 1987) which play a role in shaping the ways that individuals choose to practise their freedom. Challenging pathologisation and the overly formulaic nature of the more mainstream therapeutic systems is certainly radical in some way. I am also sure that these therapies can be considered useful for many persons, not least in their mode of LGBT affirmative treatment. However, I am arguing that these approaches while basing themselves on a challenge to power never really got to grips with the broader, structural issues of power and hierarchy in the first place. That is, while they place more emphasis on relational rather than individual problems, they still fail to account for the role of broader structures of power and inequality, and at the same time fail to reflect on the possibility that therapeutic practices constitute a form of regulatory discourse, in other words, even constructionist approaches still shape and reshape clients self-understandings and concomitantly their conduct. However, if we instead focus on this shaping and reshaping via the authority of therapeutic/counselling discourse, a new set of issues emerges. In particular, it invites not only a focus on the detailed content of the therapeutic exchange, in particular the novel forms that clients' discourses take during and at the end of therapy/counselling, but also a focus on the potentially oppressive structures and forms of understanding (for example, heterosexist, heteropatriarchal) that impact on the ways we assemble our identities. These understandings and structures not only relate to categories such as lesbian, gay, trans and queer (including what we might term queer narratives and accounts of self) but fundamentally to the predominant ways through which we understand ourselves as sexual and desiring beings.

Conclusion: queer dilemmas

I have argued in this chapter that if we wish to properly engage with Queer Theory then we need to be open to the idea that therapy constitutes the operation of a micro-power, a productive means of shaping subjectivity and conduct which is inevitably linked to broader relations of power, for example biopower, capitalism (and ultimately our contemporary moral and ethical universe). Counselling and therapy in this model do not work by giving or taking power to or from clients but rather provide a new ethical map (including a new vocabulary) that enables individuals to work upon themselves, that is, providing novel ways for clients to practise their freedom. In so doing clients become aligned not only with psychological expertise but also with a kind of authority, one based on therapeutic principles of autonomy, responsibility and self-governance. What then does this mean for practice? Foucault's model does not assume that therapy is inherently good or bad but rather asks us to understand its operation in a new way. We can ask to what extent is therapeutic practice about re-aligning the marginalised with mainstream societal values and needs? To what extent are counsellors and therapists the conduits between therapeutic authority and individual bodies?

I suggest that Queer Theory and especially Foucauldian analyses, rather than providing a concrete model of alternative practice, in fact present a range of dilemmas for contemporary psychotherapy and counselling. The question of how practitioners might deal with these dilemmas is not amenable to easy answers. Queer Theory itself embodies many contradictions and ambivalences. For example, while it has been shown that reclaiming terms such as queer, turning them back to face the oppressors, can be very effective – both in galvanising action and enabling resistance to authority – such reclamation does not allow for control over how these terms are used. Just as the term gay – claimed as a positive, liberatory identification – has also become a slur (witness school children announcing 'that's so gay' as a generic condemnation), the term queer may also outlive its usefulness as oppositional and transcendent.

Cohen (1997) convincingly argues that to be queer is fundamentally to be *alienated* socially, economically and politically, and thus she claims that the term queer may therefore apply to many individuals beyond those who are members of sexual minorities, including those who may identify as straight but are marginalised through class or race and ethnicity. It is important then, to remember that the key tenets of Queer Theory and activism are first, its opposition and resistance to power and authority – including the power to define (categorise) who we are and the concomitant moral judgements concerning conduct – and, second, its attempts to re-imagine our relationships with ourselves and with others, fundamentally its attempt to re-invent our ethical and moral universe. Thus, it is resistance to power and authority coupled with the opening up of less oppressive and less marginalising ethical and moral spaces which marks out queer practices rather than an investment in the term queer itself.

It is possible from the arguments above to briefly identify two major dilemmas for a 'queering' of therapeutic practice, though there are of course many more. First, there is the issue of how we deal with identity categories in LGBT affirmative therapy and therapeutic practice in general. It is commonly held that affirming LGBT identity is a positive therapeutic goal, but we could ask for whom? If a client has trouble or even refuses to identify as LGBT does this mean they are failing to deal with their own homophobia? Or should we see this as a positive sign of (queer) resistance? How would we know the difference?

For example, in my experience of working in self-help groups with men who are struggling to come out, it is very common for clients to resist the labels gay and bi. There is a very fine line here between encouraging clients to question negative stereotypes and assumptions (this is a very important function of such groups) and *promoting* an alignment with established identity categories. For example, how should we intervene with a client who displays a very negative and homophobic view of himself and who at the same time strongly rejects identity categories such as gay and bi as restrictive labels, which I have found commonplace in these groups? It is easy from a therapeutic viewpoint, and not unreasonable, to link these rejections to the client's own rejection of their unwanted impulses/desires. However, a Queer perspective invites us to question this. If a client is struggling to even say the words 'I am gay' or 'I am lesbian', does it make sense to question identity categories such as these and encourage clients to think of themselves as queer – a term which for many of the clients I see would be much more threatening. Is it possible to challenge clients' internalised homophobia while at the same time challenging labels such as lesbian and gay? In the groups I have mentioned we encourage clients to label themselves (if at all) in any way that is meaningful and comfortable for them. However, they will ultimately try to find ways to make their own sense of their desires and to share and communicate this with others, thus at some point they will require the words to say it. Thus, again we are back with the centrality of the spoken content of our interventions and the complex relation between our private understandings of who we are and who we desire and the ways these are moulded and regulated by power and authority (including the power of counselling and therapy). In other words, what is required is a thoroughgoing examination of what we say to clients and the effects of our talk including the implicit, taken-for-granted values, assumptions, beliefs and images we are conveying – the particular models of the 'good', 'fully functioning', 'effective' persons we are deploying.

The example above reflects some of the conflicts of past and current sexual politics. To what extent should we affirm sameness or difference, assimilation or revolution, as members of minority groups? As I have argued, the issue here is to what extent we should rally around (LGBT) identity as liberatory categories. In which instances could this be therapeutic, would it be counter-therapeutic in some cases? Here Queer Theory, I suggest, opens up a variety of ways to think about and discuss the complexity of LGBT identities where these categories are (variously) recognised, empowered, vilified, admired, ghettoised, trivialised, dismissed, and heavily invested with emotions, including shame and pride, love and hate, desire and disgust. Queer Theory, as I outlined above, at a minimum provides a warning about investing too much in identity categories, and it is power and authority that ultimately need to be recognised and worked through in our therapeutic practices; however, we cannot achieve this by assuming we are able to hand our power back to clients. Even the, for some, groundbreaking work of Michael White and David Epston (1992), while making major advances in bringing the ideas of Foucault and others into therapeutic practice – especially through relocating problems outside the individual, a process they term externalisation – provide very little concrete reflection on the effects of their own discursive practices/interventions and the pivotal role of authority for the efficacy of their approach. For me Queer Theory is above all about insubordination – the question is can we use therapy as a mode of resistance? And if so, how?

Thus, the second key dilemma relates to how we deal with our (discursive) power as therapists and counsellors. In particular, if the therapeutic conversation, in some sense, aligns individuals with contemporary modes of authority, even at the very moment they affirm their innermost truths, then can and should we resist this in our therapeutic practices? Put another way, could (or should) we resist therapeutic authority and still practise therapy or counselling? Here I have shown that rather than individualising power we need ultimately to re-invent (in Butler's words to redeploy, to twist, to queer) – and this would need to occur at the levels of community and society – the ethical spaces and relations (that is, the ways in which the self relates to itself, is made accountable to itself), that enable us to assemble and re-assemble ourselves as ethical beings (including our relations to others and our communities). That is, we need to re-invent new modes and formations for the care of the self. It is here that the recognition of queer accounts and queer narratives, that is narratives which, for example, explore the relations between social, cultural and economic structures and individual experiences such as alienation.

Thus we must carefully attend to the practices we invite clients to adopt, the problematic aspects of themselves we are helping them construct, the various forms of therapeutic work these require and especially the ends towards which the therapeutic encounter leads. In other words, it is primarily therapeutic discourse that needs to be changed rather than the attitudes, sense of responsibility and motivations of the therapist (though these do, of course, play a role). These practices could in the first instance be clarified through detailed analysis of our therapeutic conversations. However in order to re-invent the ethical spaces we open up, and perhaps in some way move them on from the therapeutic authority described here, we need to collectively and creatively use our imaginations. Perhaps, taking our example from queer activism, it is only through collective action – including action through the various communities of professional counsellors and therapists – that these issues can be properly and meaningfully addressed. It only makes sense to engage Queer Theory with therapeutic practices if we believe that therapy is not only a means through which we may engender changes in psychic structures but also a means through which the structures of inequality in society and culture may be challenged and transformed. That is, only if we believe that counselling and therapy are thoroughly political practices.

Notes

1 The distinction between counselling and psychotherapy is an important one, not least because there are a variety of explanations offered in the literature. On the whole, however, a separation between the two is considered somewhat illusory while certain differences in overall aims (Patterson 1995: xvii) or 'client populations and settings' (Nelson-Jones 1992:3) are, for example, acknowledged. Here I refer to counselling and psychotherapeutic practices together, assuming that both target (elements of) the 'self' as a site of transformation, but where generalisations from one to the other must be made with some caution.

2 From its birth, Queer Theory (see Norton, 1997, for a useful history of the term queer) was linked to political movements which included Queer Nation in the US (and to a lesser extent the UK), Outrage in London and Homocult in Manchester.

3 Key early queer texts included Judith Butler's (1991) *Gender Trouble* and (1993) *Bodies that Matter*, Jonathon Dollimore's (1991) *Sexual Dissidence*, Michel Foucault's (1990b) *History of Sexuality*, Vol. 1, Eve Sedgewick's (1990) *Epistemology of the Closet*, Cherry Smyth's (1992) *Lesbians Talk Queer Notions* and Michael Warner's (1993) *Fear of a Queer Planet*.

4 Foucault used the term biopolitics to refer to the complex technical operation of power upon bodies and populations, 'By [biopolitics] I mean the endeavour, begun in the eighteenth century, to rationalise the problems presented to governmental practice by the phenomena characteristic of a group of living human beings constituted as a population: health, sanitation, birth-rate, longevity, race. . .' (Foucault in Rabinow 1994:73).

5 Section or Clause 28 refers to an amendment to the Local Government Act 1986 which took place in May 1988 initiated by the then Conservative government under Margaret Thatcher. It was eventually repealed in November 2003. The amendment stated:

> (1) A Local Authority shall not
>   (a) intentionally promote homosexuality or publish material with the intention of promoting homosexuality;
>   (b) promote the teaching in any maintained school of the acceptability of homosexuality as a pretended family relationship.

While no one was ever successfully prosecuted under this clause, it produced a climate of fear across the public sector, especially in schools, where teachers no longer felt able to freely discuss LGB issues in the classroom. Groups and services for LGB persons were forced to close because of fears of prosecution and/or removal of funding. Many at the time felt this clause was deeply homophobic and the recent campaign for its repeal met with challenge.

References

Anderson, H. and Goolishian, H. (1992) The client is the expert: a not-knowing approach to therapy. In S. MacNamee and K. Gergen (eds), *Therapy as Social Construction*. London: Sage, pp. 25–39.

Anonymous. (1990) *Queers Read This*. A leaflet distributed at pride march in New York. Published anonymously by Queers. [Online] http://www.qrd.org/qrd/misc/text/queers.read.this [accessed May 2007].

Bateson, G. (1972) *Steps to an Ecology of Mind: Collected Essays in Anthropology, Psychiatry, Evolution and Epistemiology*. Chicago: Chicago University Press.

Butler, J. (1991) *Gender Trouble: Feminism and the Subversion of Identity*. London: Routledge.

Butler, J. (1993) *Bodies That Matter: On the Discursive Limits of Sex*. London: Routledge.

Cohen, C. (1997) Punks, bulldaggers, and welfare queens: the radical potential of queer politics. *GLQ: A Journal of Lesbian and Gay Studies*, **3**, 437–65.

Dollimore, J. (1991) *Sexual Dissidence: Augustine to Wilde, Freud to Foucault*. Oxford: Oxford University Press.

Foucault, M. (1980) The confession of the flesh. In C. Gordon (ed.), *Power/Knowledge: Selected Interviews and Other Writings 1972–1977 by Michel Foucault*. Hemel Hempstead: Harvester Wheatsheaf, pp. 196–228.

Foucault, M. (1988) Technologies of the self. In L. Martin, H. Gutman, and P. Hutton (eds), *Technologies of the Self: A Seminar with Michel Foucault*. London: Tavistock, pp. 16–49.

Foucault, M. (1990a) 'Practising criticism' or 'Is it really important to think?' Interview by Didier Eribon, May 30–31, 1981. In L. Kritzman (ed.), *Michel Foucault, Politics, Power and Culture: Interviews and Other Writings 1977–1984*. London: Routledge, pp. 152–6.

Foucault, M. (1990b) *The History of Sexuality: An Introduction, vol. 1*. London: Penguin.

Foucault, M. (1991) Governmentality. In G. Burchell, C. Gordon, and P. Miller (eds), *The Foucault Effect: Studies in Governmentality*. Hemel Hempstead: Harvester Wheatsheaf, pp. 87–104.

Foucault, M. (1992) *The History of Sexuality: The Use of Pleasure, vol. 2*. London: Penguin.

Fruggeri, L. (1992) Therapeutic process as the social construction of change. In S. MacNamee and K. Gergen (eds), *Therapy as Social Construction*. London: Sage.

Gergen, K. (1985) The social constructionist movement in modern social psychology. *American Psychologist*, **40**, 266–75.

Gergen, K. (1992) Toward a postmodern psychology. In S. Kvale (ed.), *Psychology and Postmodernism*. London: Sage, pp. 17–30.

Hodges, I. (1998) A problem aired: exploring radio therapeutic discourse and ethical self-formation. Unpublished PhD thesis, Goldsmiths, University of London.

Hodges, I. (2001) A problem aired: radio therapeutic discourse and modes of subjection. In J. Morss, N. Stephenson and H. Van Rappard (eds), *Theoretical Issues in Psychology*. Berlin: Springer, pp. 351–66.

Hodges, I. (2002) Moving beyond words: therapeutic discourse and ethical problematisation. *Discourse Studies*, **4**, 455–79.

Hodges, I. (2003) Broadcasting the audience: radio therapeutic discourse and its implied listeners. *International Journal of Critical Psychology*, **7**, 74–101.

Miller, P. (1987) *Domination and Power*. London: Routledge & Kegan Paul.

Nelson-Jones, R. (1992) *The Theory and Practice of Counselling Psychology*. London: Cassell.

Norton, R. (1997) *The Myth of the Modern Homosexual*. London: Cassell.

Patterson, C.H. (1995) *Theories of Counselling and Psychotherapy*. New York: Harper Collins.

Rabinow, P. (1994) *Ethics: The Essential Works of Foucault 1954–1984*, vol. 1. London: Penguin.

Rose, N. (1985) *The Psychological Complex: Psychology, Politics and Society in England 1869–1939*. London: Routledge & Kegan Paul.

Rose, N. (1990) *Governing the Soul: The Shaping of the Private Self*. London: Routledge.

Rose, N. (1992) *Towards a Critical Sociology of Freedom: Inaugural Lecture, Goldsmiths College, 5th May 1992*. London: Goldsmiths College.

Rose, N. (1996) *Inventing Ourselves: Psychology, Power and Personhood*. Cambridge: Cambridge University Press.

Rose, N. (1998) *Power in Therapy: Techne and Ethos*. Academy for the Study of the Psychoanalytic Arts. [Online] www.academyanalyticarts.org/rose2.htm [accessed May 2007].

Sedgewick, E. (1990) *Epistemology of the Closet*. Hemel Hempstead: Harvester Wheatsheaf.

Simon, G. and Whitfield, G. (2000) Systemic and social constructionist therapy. In D. Davies (ed.), *Pink Therapy II. Theoretical Approaches to Work with Lesbians, Gay Men, Bbisexual and Transgender People*. London: Open University Press, pp. 101–25.

Smyth, C. (1992) *Lesbians Talk Queer Notions*. London: Scarlett Press.

Warner, M. (1993) *Fear of a Queer Planet: Queer Politics and Social Theory*. Minneapolis: University of Minnesota Press.

White, M. and Epston, D. (1992) *Narrative Means to Therapeutic Ends*. London: W. Norton.

Chapter 3

Are you angry or are you heterosexual?

A queer critique of lesbian and gay models of identity development

Darren Langdridge

'Are you angry or are you boring?' screams one of Gilbert and Georges' dirty words pictures.[1] I want to take this as my theme in this chapter as I offer a queer critique of dominant lesbian, gay and bisexual (LGB) coming-out models (Cass 1979; Coleman 1981/1982; Troiden 1979; Woodman and Lena 1980) in use in counselling and psychotherapy today. These models present particular difficulties when working with LGB and especially queer (Q) clients as they incorporate a belief that successful coming out involves a move towards a fixed and stable identity and quiet acceptance of the wider social world. Building on my previous work on hermeneutic phenom-enology, sexualities and psychotherapy (Langdridge 2003, 2004, 2006, in press), this chapter will critique stage models, focusing in particular on the model of Cass (1979), bringing together key ideas from hermeneutics and queer theory. In particular, I will argue that instead of aiming for fixity, we should engage with a radical queer hermeneutic of suspicion (Ricoeur 1970), aim for flexibility and furthermore, that the endpoint of coming out should not be quiet contentment with one's self and one's social world but appropriate and justifiable anger at the endemic heterosexism and homo-negativity in the late modern world.[2]

First, I will outline the Cass Identity Model (Cass 1979, 1984), which is one of the most widely known and well-used models of lesbian and gay identity development (Ritter and Terndrup 2002). I will use the model as an exemplar of stage models, all of which specify a particular developmental path for lesbians and gay men. Following this, I will discuss some of the criticisms of such stage models, including the concern that they do not represent the experience of the broader LGBTQ community and also that they serve to fix the developmental experience in a linear progressive form. The chapter will then introduce queer theory and use concepts from this theoretical perspective to critique stage models of LGBTQ development. Finally, I will introduce ideas from Ricoeur's (1970) philosophy and, in particular, his distinction between hermeneutics of meaning-recollection and suspicion. I will use these ideas to outline a way of working in a strong gay affirmative way with clients (Langdridge in press) enabling therapists to work in a critical queer way with the client and social world into which they are thrown. With this in mind, the end point of 'successful' identity development need not be contentment – which is not only politically conservative but also boring – as is currently the norm, but rather anger at the heterosexism and homophobia still prevalent in contemporary culture.

The Cass Identity Model

Vivienne Cass first proposed her model of homosexual identity formation ('coming out') in 1979. She describes six stages of identity formation based on two fundamental assumptions that: (1) identity formation is a developmental process and (2) stability and change in behaviour lies in the interaction between the individual and their environment. The model is therefore linear and interactionist, founded on the notion that identity development proceeds in a linear fashion (c.f. Erikson 1946) and furthermore that development (or not) is the result of an interaction between individuals and the social world. The model resulted from clinical work with 'homosexuals'. I focus on this particular stage model in this chapter but the critique is also applicable to all other stage models of identity development. The Cass model led to a proliferation of other psychological (e.g. Coleman 1981/1982; Troiden 1979; Woodman and Lena 1980) and sociological (e.g. Plummer 1995) models of sexual identity development, many of which remain influential amongst psychological and sociological theorists as well as amongst practitioners (see, for instance, Davies 1996). In many ways, these models reflect social (and sexual) life in this particular period of history through the twin implicit assumptions of linear development and stable (sexual) identities that underpin them. It is only with more recent socio-cultural critiques – such as that from queer theory – that questions have been raised about their theoretical basis and practical utility. This chapter aims to highlight the limitations of such models and also provide possible ways forward for practitioners who recognise that critical alternatives may be needed if we are to engage with the political world in our clinical practice.

The theoretical heart of the Cass model is interpersonal congruency theory (Secord and Backman 1961), which proposes that individual stability and change are dependent on the degree of congruence or incongruence between an individual and their environment. Cass (1979) uses this theory to understand movement or non-movement from one stage to another. That is, movement occurs as a result of some incongruence between the individual and their environment as a result of that individual assigning homosexual meaning to their own feelings, thoughts or behaviours. For Cass (1979:220), 'Growth occurs when P attempts to resolve the inconsistency between perception of self and others'. However, foreclosure can occur at any stage with people remaining 'stuck' in one of the earlier five stages and not ever reaching identity synthesis (the sixth stage).

Cass's six stages are:

(1) Identity confusion

The first stage of identity development comes through increasing awareness of the personal salience of information about homosexuality. With this awareness there is a realisation that one's own thoughts, feelings or behaviours can be labelled as homosexual with this knowledge eventually being impossible to ignore. This is the first moment of incongruence as the individual's perception of self as heterosexual is at odds with their own perception of their thoughts, feelings or behaviour. As a result, the individual experiences confusion and is forced to ask themselves whether they might be homosexual.

(2) Identity comparison

By the end of stage 1, the person should have moved from a belief that they are heterosexual to one where they *might be* homosexual. Stage 2 involves a change away from an immediate concern with personal identity to a concern with the social alienation that may be perceived. The continuity between a person's past, present and future has now been broken, and they must find new meaning in life. This occurs because many of the expectations placed upon the person have changed and/or become irrelevant (such as marrying and setting up a family). A number of possible responses are available including feeling positive about one's identity, 'passing' as a heterosexual, resisting opportunities to behave homosexually (while recognising that they are homosexual), and self-hatred leading to a desire to change orientation.

(3) Identity tolerance

At this stage, the person is beginning to recognise that they are probably homosexual and as such begin to seek out contact with other homosexuals to reduce the sense of alienation they are feeling. There is not acceptance though, just tolerance, and the quality of the contact with others is crucial in enabling movement from this stage to the next. Good quality contacts, where the individual feels recognised and valued, alongside a sense of belonging, are important in enabling them to accept their identity. However, contacts which are perceived negatively by someone who already feels negatively about their homosexual thoughts and feelings may result in the devaluation of the homosexual subculture and either reduction of contact or inhibition of all homosexual behaviours.

(4) Identity acceptance

At this stage the person has come to accept their sexual identity and continues to make contact with other homosexuals. People will develop a preference for homosexual social contexts, and friendships will develop. Passing will become less common as selective disclosure of sexual identity occurs.

(5) Identity pride

Here the individual feels their identity is completely acceptable and indeed the source of some pride. There is recognition that it is society that is wrong to condemn homosexuality and that they are not sick or ill. Contact with the homosexual community is maximised, but friendships only really exist amongst other homosexuals. Alongside this pride comes anger at the homophobia of heterosexual people and society.

(6) Identity synthesis

This final stage involves recognition that the 'them and us' strategy, in which all heterosexuals are viewed negatively and all homosexuals positively, is no longer true. There is maximum congruency between a person's feelings, thoughts, behaviour and environment. The person also accepts the possibility of considerable similarity between themselves and heterosexuals. Finally, a person's identity becomes merely one aspect of their notion of selfhood rather than their whole identity.

Evidence and extant critique

Cass (1984) herself sought to empirically validate her model of identity development by conducting a survey of 178 people recruited from a wide variety of sources including counselling services for 'homosexuals', newspaper adverts, personal contacts etc. Cass found some support for her model but also evidence for the blurring of stages, most notably between stages 1 and 2, and stages 5 and 6. There were also differences between men and women indicating that the model may need to be revised. More recently, Halpin and Allen (2004) sought to evaluate Cass's model amongst 425 men recruited through the internet by ascertaining whether psychosocial well-being improved through the six stages. They found that well-being was high during the initial confusion and comparison stages, reduced during the middle tolerance and acceptance stages and high again in the final pride and synthesis stages providing some validation for the model.

The model, and others like it, has also been the subject of criticism on the grounds that it fails to

(1) sufficiently differentiate male and female experience
(2) account for bisexuality
(3) recognise the complex interplay of individual and social world – notably through an understanding of the biography of the individual and reality of their environmental context
(4) recognise that identity development is a continual lifetime process and
(5) acknowledge that the six stages do not necessarily fit the lived experience of large numbers of lesbians and gay men (see, for instance, Horowitz and Newcomb 2001).

It remains powerful – along with several others – however, not simply for the way it appeals to counsellors and psychotherapists seeking to understand the process of coming out but also because it does not simply describe the process of coming out – as is professed – but contributes to the construction of a particular process through the active proliferation of this story of coming out. The media (factual and fictional), counsellors, psychotherapists and psychologists, amongst others, act to encourage this particular story, which is then taken up by young men and women questioning their identity and finding recognition of their private pain in this very public story (Plummer 1995). While this may act to alleviate the private quality of the pain being felt, it may also serve to prematurely foreclose other possible ways of living, which may better suit the experience of the individual now or later.

Queer theory and LGBTQ development

Queer theory is hard to define but is concerned with disrupting binary categories of identity and therefore providing a radical challenge to many of the assumptions underpinning common-sense understandings of self and identity, in the West at least. It has been used as an overarching term for all work concerning lesbian, gay, bisexual and trans identities as well as a term for a theoretical perspective focused on transgression and rebellion (Seidman 1996). However, in this context, I understand queer theory as a perspective which challenges the notion of a unified homosexual (or indeed heterosexual) identity (Butler 1990). Most work in LGBT psychology, especially that concerned with identity development, has assumed a homosexual subject with discussion and debate centred on the origin, role and meaning of subjectivity for the homosexual. Queer theorists have drawn on work by black radicals and sexual dissidents, along with the poststructuralist critique of language as representation, to argue that identities are always multiple, unstable and regulatory.

However, in spite of the fact that queer theory has had a significant impact on many disciplines in the arts and humanities, and some, though less, impact on such social sciences as sociology and anthropology, its impact on psychology has been extremely limited. Much of this is to do with the way in which psychology has sought to embrace a natural science model of human nature, eschewing interpretivism, and post-modern critiques. However, since the crisis in social psychology in the 1970s, psychology has had to engage with the many critical challenges that have come its way. This has most obviously included the challenge from feminist theory, which has led to a radical transformation of some, though by no means all, sections of the discipline.

If one applies the principles of queer theory to models of identity development like that of Cass, then the modernist notions implied in such theories are highlighted and challenged. The principal challenge to such models comes from the critique of fixed categories of identity. With a fixed identity category such as 'homosexual', comes a necessary 'othering' by the dominant centre, heterosexuality. As such, no matter what rights are won (and considerable rights have indeed been won of late) the homosexual will always remain outside, other to the norm that is the insider: that is, other than the heterosexual. The homosexual will always therefore be less than the heterosexual, perilously dependent on the good will of the heterosexual for their continued rights. Queer theory seeks to undermine this heterosexual–homosexual binary by actively refusing to engage with identity categories and actively affirming ambiguity. The aim therefore of fixity, of a firm resolved homosexual identity at the heart of the Cass model, and many others, is challenged for the way it both limits possible ways of being and also critically for the way it reinforces and reifies heterosexual and homosexual identities.

The quiet acceptance that comes with identity synthesis might also be critically queered: For there is something very conservative and reasonable about such a position, something which makes me distinctly uncomfortable. Queer politics, on the other hand, has often been difficult and bitchy, uncompromising and radical, with an active refusal to accept the status quo, to be a 'good citizen' (Bell and Binnie 2000). The political position implied by the quiet acceptance of congruence between the homosexual and heterosexual worlds belies the intrinsic differences in power and authority accrued with these identities. Heterosexuality is privileged and heterosexism and homonegativity are pervasive, serving to reinforce this privilege. The way power is encoded in these relations needs to be highlighted and not ignored for the way it is employed to serve the needs of one group of people over another. We do not need happy acceptance – that must remain the province of heterosexuality – but rather anger, appropriate and justifiable anger, at the endemic heterosexism and homonegativity that still exists in this late modern world.

The need for a hermeneutic of suspicion

But just how do we engage in practice with queer theory? How can we work with such a radical position when therapist and client are both immersed in modernist notions of sex, gender and sexual identity development. Here, I propose one way of engaging with these ideas that respects existing practice while recognising the need for socio-political critique. I do not propose a wholesale queering of the psychotherapeutic project here, but rather a critical adaptation enabling client and therapist to bring the political clearly and directly into the therapeutic arena. I focus on existential and humanistic therapies here, as they represent my speciality, but also because they occupy a central place in the development of gay affirmative practice and work with lesbian, gay, bisexual and queer clients.

Existential and humanistic psychotherapies rightly concentrate on the hermeneutic of meaning-recollection (or empathy). That is, priority is always given to the experience as expressed by the client. Clients are trusted and respected for the way in which they are responsible for their own lives. Psychoanalysis and psychoanalytic psychotherapies, however, concentrate on a hermeneutic of suspicion (Ricoeur 1970). Here, priority is given to uncovering hidden meaning, discovering the truth that lies beneath. This, of course, presents the danger of an excess of suspicion, where the client's agency is subjugated to that of the therapist. Famously, in Freudian theory, the client is not master in their own house, and with this the analyst assumes a position of power and authority, since they believe they have knowledge about the client and their way of experiencing that is not available to them. I think it would be a retrograde step to reject the hermeneutic of meaning-recollection at the heart of existential and humanistic practice and instead embrace a hermeneutic of suspicion. However, I believe the desire of existential and humanistic psychotherapists to maintain a distance from psychoanalysis and psychoanalytic psychotherapy – to diverge from their origins – has meant they have failed to see the positive potential of a hermeneutic of suspicion, especially a queer hermeneutic which challenges modernist notions of sexual identity and identity development.

But what is the positive potential? Perhaps the most important argument for using a hermeneutic of suspicion concerns the positive potential to use it to counter the oppression resulting from particular (often hidden) discourses and subject positions. We are all embedded in cultural discourses, some of which are not apparent and as such hidden from the analytic gaze. By incorporating a degree of suspicion a therapist may be able to act as critic, raising the client's consciousness about the situated nature of their subjectivity. Perhaps the clearest contemporary examples here come from the realm of social movements. The feminist and lesbian, gay and bisexual movements have demonstrated the power of discourses to oppress and the need for consciousness-raising on the part of those who have been oppressed. When oppressive discourses have been internalised as a form of self-surveillance (Foucault 1977), it is very hard for the oppressed to resist, since the first step in resistance is awareness of being oppressed and knowledge of the possibility of living differently. Enabling people to see different ways of living is, of course, the *raison d'être* of social movements and, I believe, should be part – though obviously not all – of the practice of psychotherapy. Deleuze and Guattari (1984) argue that all psychotherapy is inherently political, marginal, subversive and even potentially revolutionary. Because even if a therapist chooses not to engage with socio-political issues directly and explicitly with a client they are still making a political choice: a choice for the status quo.

Suspicion can come from many sources but the hermeneutic of suspicion that I am advocating here is not a depth hermeneutic like psychoanalysis. Instead, while employing the distinction between hermeneutics of meaning-recollection (the usual project of existential and humanistic psychotherapies) and suspicion initiated by Ricoeur (1970), I make a further distinction between hermeneutic types (see Langdridge 2006). Specifically, I distinguish between two types of hermeneutic of suspicion: *imaginative* and *depth hermeneutics*. Depth hermeneutics are those methods of interpretation founded on the notion of needing to dig beneath the surface for deeper meaning, often, though not always, concealed from the subject who is the focus of the investigation. The classic depth hermeneutic is of course psychoanalytic theory. Here, when applied to the therapeutic process, the analyst looks for clues in the countertransference indicating what they perceive to be unconscious dynamics, such as clients defending themselves against anxiety or projecting aspects of themselves onto others.

Imaginative hermeneutics of suspicion are, by contrast, a way of moving beyond a simple focus on the apparent, through critical engagement with the social world into which client and therapist are thrown, while not subsuming the meanings of the participant to the analyst. Here, I suggest that instead of digging beneath the surface for hidden meaning not apparent to the client, one engages in a critical form of imaginative variation, using ideas from appropriate social theories and/or socio-political critique. That is, by employing specific hermeneutics, the therapist aims to enable the client to gain an alternative way of seeing, not a way which reveals the truth hidden beneath the surface, but rather a way of taking up an alternative position – recognising that we always have a view from somewhere (Ricoeur 1984) within existing ideological structures – and, therefore, enabling a critical move beyond the apparent. This move does not involve the therapist offering a superior interpretation, but rather encouraging a *perspectival shift* in understandings of the lifeworld through a critical interrogation of the social imaginary (Ricoeur 1984) of narratives the client inhabits and, therefore, reproduces naturally in the stories they tell of their lives. The claim is not to have grasped some hidden 'truth' about the person, as one might with depth hermeneutics of suspicion, but rather to offer up an alternative perspective on the phenomena and specifically an alternative grounded in broader socio-cultural discourse. The move is *temporarily* from a focus on the lifeworld of the client and their meanings to a critical analysis of the narrative world that both allows and limits their ways of speaking about the world. Offering up an alternative reading is therefore designed to open up possible ways of living, which may or may not be taken up by the client. I believe that this theoretical perspective, which employs an imaginative, rather than depth, hermeneutic provides a way forward for existential and humanistic theory and practice which recognises the need for political critique, opening up new ways of narrating a life story (Ricoeur 1992), without imposing deterministic frameworks of meaning on to the client.

The case being made here is that it is necessary to engage in a multi-layered (empathic and suspicious) analysis of all discourse. That is, *both* client and therapist should be subjected to a *demythologising* (or empathic) process *and* a *demystifying* (or suspicious) process. By recognising the therapist's own role in recovering meaning within the therapeutic encounter, and then putting this forward for criticism along with the interpretation of the client, the client should themselves act as co-critic of the illusions of subjectivity. A critical part of the work with any client therefore must be to empower them to act in this way: as a sceptic, as a co-critic, as an equal. Should too much of the therapist be projected into the therapeutic encounter, a sceptical client will not find the meaning-recollection persuasive or resonant. Too little and the therapist and client may find themselves limited to an empathic engagement with little or no suspicion about the client or social world into which both are thrown.

Destabilising a narrative like this involves the therapist directly engaging in political critique or deconstruction (Derrida 1976). The need for a hermeneutic of suspicion when engaged in meaning-recollection is controversial, but potentially very important in countering the dangers of a naïve phenomenology. As Ricoeur (1981) makes clear in his intervention in the debate between Gadamer and Habermas, we can never have 'a view from nowhere'. That is, we always speak from somewhere, from some tradition and some ideological position. A phenomenological perspective arguing for a transcendental subject able to situate itself outside all ideological positions is naïve (Langdridge 2004). For, not only are we physically situated and contingent but also socially, culturally and politically situated and contingent (Ricoeur 1981). We can try to bracket our preconceptions and recollect meaning from our clients, but this will always be imperfect. This does not mean we should abandon this aim, but perhaps it reminds us of the need to be honest about, and mindful of, the situated nature of the therapist.

Here the therapist needs to complete the hermeneutic circle. This process is explicitly political and requires the therapist to engage with critical social theories and/or other socio-political material to enable them to work with the client to critique the discursive boundaries in which they are situated. If one accepts the need to critique the illusions of the subject, and to subject the client's story to an imaginative hermeneutic of suspicion as well as a hermeneutic of meaning-recollection, then the question arises about what specific hermeneutic should be employed in the work. Any number of hermeneutics may be relevant depending on the context. Ideas from social theory, such as queer theory (Butler 1990), are possible and appropriate sources of suspicion especially when working with clients questioning their sexuality and/or gender (see Langdridge, in press, for more on the justification for using a queer hermeneutic of suspicion in affirmative practice). The choice must clearly be guided by the need of the client, therapeutic judgement and socio-political position of the therapist.

Queer therapy in practice

This final section seeks to demonstrate how a queer hermeneutic of suspicion might be applied during the course of the therapeutic work with a client presenting with confusion over his sexual identity.

> Javier, a twenty-two-year-old Hispanic male, came to see me as he was having difficulties in his relationship with his girlfriend, Claire. Javier came from a very traditional background, which left him with a strong set of beliefs about how he should be as a man. In particular, he felt he should be strong, emotionally and physically, the main money earner and dominant member of the couple. This was, however, at odds with Javier's lived experience, since he found himself to be emotionally labile, not particularly physically strong, and in a relationship with a woman who was much more educated and earned considerably more money than he did. He also, rather crucially, recognised that he found men emotionally and sexually attractive. His lived experience was therefore in tension with his belief system – in many ways an apparently internalised representation of his parents' belief system rather than his own. Javier did not believe himself to be gay and was quite clear about his love and sexual attraction for his girlfriend. He did, however, recognise that his own worries about his masculinity and sexuality were leading to unnecessary conflict in his relationship.

Anger and frustration emerged as a consequence of the incongruity between his experience and beliefs, much as one might expect from the model of development proposed by Cass (1979). However, in this case the problem centred around the fixity of his identity as a heterosexual (which might equally have been problematic had his identity been fixed as homosexual). Neither a heterosexual nor homosexual identity served to make Javier's lived experience congruent with his belief system. His lived experience was such that he felt a constant challenge to what Sartre (1939/ 2002) terms the *hodological map* – the mental map of the paths which we believe we will follow to reach our goals, and through which we see the world before us as if it were of our own making – and what was vital was the need to redraw this map so it was more in line with Javier's lived experience rather than constantly finding himself frustrated when it was at odds with his desires.

Over the course of our work I sought to gradually bring in a queer hermeneutic of suspicion. As always, my work was first and foremost phenomenological (Langdridge 2006), seeking to understand Javier's lived experience, but with time and lack of change on his part, I felt it appropriate to act as a critic of hegemonic masculinity and fixed notions of sexual identity. This came about through direct psycho-education about gender and sexuality and strategic challenges to his extant hodological map. References to it being 'natural' or 'necessary' for men to be dominant and heterosexual were actively challenged and the possibility of finding ways of living in which we do not label ourselves homosexual or heterosexual were actively articulated. Javier resisted at first, as I expected, but came to embrace these possibilities over time with reflection upon his life and desires. He did not therefore work towards identity synthesis but rather towards an ambiguity with regard to his sexuality, which better reflected his lived experience and desires about how he wanted to live. Javier found himself increasingly satisfied with the relationship he had and his other sex desires, feeling more content with his gender and resisting the need to label himself in any particular way. He also became able to talk his feelings through with his girlfriend which reduced the conflict in their relationship and, finally, with these changes he was able to realise a new hodological map, which was more congruent with the lived experience of his gender and sexuality.

Conclusion

In this chapter I have sought to highlight the limitations of stage models of identity development, such as that of Cass (1979), and provide a critical alternative that employs ideas from queer theory. To this end, I first outlined Cass's (1979) model of coming out. I then discussed the limitations of such a model, including the possibility of such a model leading to the premature foreclosure of the variety of lived experience amongst lesbian, gay, bisexual and queer people. I then introduced some fundamental ideas from queer theory and discussed how these provide a radical challenge to models which describe, and implicitly prescribe, a fixed identity and happy acceptance of the social world as the final (ideal) state of identity development. Finally, I introduced Ricoeur's (1970) notion of a hermeneutic of suspicion and how this might be a way – theoretically speaking – of employing queer theory in existential and humanistic psychotherapeutic practice. This radical move recognises and works with the knowledge of our situated positions as client and therapist and the impact of the social world on our understandings of self and others, while never subjugating the lived experience of the client to the political ambitions of the therapist. The aim of sexual identity development and the aim of affirmative psychotherapy are – from this perspective – no longer fixity and acceptance but rather ambiguity, recognising the need to resist binary categories of identity, personally and politically, and also anger at the endemic heterosexism and homonegativity that still exists in these late modern times. With this in mind, I must ask all counsellors and psychotherapists whether the end point of 'successful' identity development should be contentment, which is not only politically conservative but also boring, as is currently the norm, or anger at the heterosexism and homophobia still prevalent in contemporary culture.

Notes

1 The Dirty Words Pictures created by Gilbert and George are multiple aggressive contrasting black and white and red images in which 'dirty' words from the environment the artists inhabited, London in the 1970s, play a key part. They were created in 1977 and first exhibited at the Serpentine Gallery in London and more recently exhibited at the same gallery in 2002. Needless to say, I am using the phrase 'Are you angry or are you heterosexual' strategically and rhetorically against the centre, reflexively mindful of the binary it sets up, such that it too needs to be subject to the same critique as any other binary.
2 I use late modern rather than postmodern to emphasise the way that at least with regard to counselling, psychology and psychotherapy, the majority of theory and practice continues to embrace modernist notions of identity and identity development – the subject of the postmodern critique presented here.

References

Bell, D. and Binnie, J. (2000). *The Sexual Citizen: Queer Politics and Beyond*. Cambridge: Polity Press.

Butler, J. (1990). *Gender Trouble*. New York, NY: Routledge.

Cass, V. (1979). Homosexual identity formation: a theoretical model. *Journal of Homosexuality*, **4**, 210–35.

Cass, V. (1984). Homosexual identity formation: testing a theoretical model. *The Journal of Sex Research*, **20**, 143–67.

Coleman, E. (1981/1982). Developmental stages of the coming out process. *Journal of Homosexuality*, **7**, 43.

Davies, D. (1996). Working with people coming out. In D. Davies and C. Neal (eds), *Pink Therapy*. Buckingham: Open University Press.

Deleuze, G. and Guattari, F. (1984). *Anti-Oedipus: Capitalism and Schizophrenia*. London: The Athlone Press.

Derrida, J. (1976). *Of Grammatology*. [Trans. G. C. Spivak] London: John Hopkins University Press.

Erikson, E. (1946). Ego development and historical change. *Psychoanalytic Study of the Child*, **2**, 359–96.

Foucault, M. (1977). *Discipline and Punish: The Birth of the Prison*. [Trans. A. Sheridan] Harmondsworth: Penguin.

Halpin, S.A. and Allen, M.W. (2004). Changes in psychosocial well-being during stages of gay identity development. *Journal of Homosexuality*, **47**, 109–26.

Horowitz, J.L. and Newcomb, M.D. (2001). A multidimensional approach to homosexual identity. *Journal of Homosexuality*, **42**, 1–19.

Langdridge, D. (2003). Hermeneutic phenomenology: arguments for a new social psychology. *History and Philosophy of Psychology*, **5**, 30–45.

Langdridge, D. (2004). The hermeneutic phenomenology of Paul Ricoeur: problems and possibilities for existential-phenomenological psychotherapy. *Existential Analysis*, **15**, 243–55.

Langdridge, D. (2006). *Phenomenological Psychology: Theory, Research and Method*. Harlow: Pearson Education.

Langdridge, D. (in press). Gay affirmative therapy: a theoretical framework and defence. In E. Peel, V. Clarke and J. Drescher (eds), *British Lesbian, Gay and Bisexual Psychologies: Theory, Research, and Practice*. New York: Haworth Press. [Simultaneous publication with *Journal of Gay & Lesbian Psychotherapy*.]

Plummer, K. (1995). *Telling Sexual Stories: Power, Change and Social Worlds*. London: Routledge.

Ricoeur, P. (1970). *Freud and Philosophy: An Essay on Interpretation*. [Trans. D. Savage]. New Haven, CT: Yale University Press.

Ricoeur, P. (1981). *Hermeneutics and the Human Sciences*. [Ed. and Trans. J.B. Thompson] Cambridge: Cambridge University Press.

Ricoeur, P. (1984). The Creativity of Language. Interview with Richard Kearney. From R. Kearney (1984) *Dialogues with Contemporary Continental Thinkers*. Manchester: Manchester University Press, pp. 17–36. Reprinted in M.J. Valdes (ed.) (1991). *A Ricoeur Reader: Reflection and Imagination*. Toronto: University of Toronto Press, pp. 463–81.

Ricoeur, P. (1992). *Oneself as Another*. [Trans. K. Blamey] Chicago: University of Chicago Press.

Ritter, K.Y. and Terndrup, A.I. (2002). *Handbook of Affirmative Psychotherapy with Lesbians and Gay Men*. New York: Guilford Press.

Sartre, J.-P. (1939/2002). *Sketch for a Theory of the Emotions*. [Trans. P. Mairet] London: Routledge.

Secord, P.F. and Backman, C.W. (1961). Personality change and the problem of stability and change in individual behavior: an interpersonal approach. *Psychological Review*, **68**, 21–32.

Seidman, S. (1996) (ed.) *Queer Theory/Sociology*. Oxford: Blackwell.

Troiden, R.R. (1979). Becoming homosexual: a model of gay identity acquisition. *Psychiatry*, **42**, 362–73.

Woodman, N.J. and Lena, H.R. (1980). *Counseling with Gay Men and Women: A Guide for Facilitating Positive Lifestyles*. San Francisco: Jossey Bass.

Chapter 4

Queer(y)ing the heterosexualisation of emotion

Lyndsey Moon

Thoughts, feelings, and actions may appear as they are the very fabric and constitution of the intimate self, but they are socially organised and managed in minute particulars.

Nikolas Rose (1989:1)

. . . we embody the discourses that exist in our culture, our very being is constituted by them, they are part of us, and thus we cannot simply throw them off.

Nikki Sullivan (2003:41)

One important aspect of queer theory is that it allows us to view the world from perspectives other than those which are generally validated by the dominant society . . . such queer(ed) positions can challenge the dominance of heterosexist discourses.

Beemyn and Eliason (1996:165)

Feelings, emotions, bodies and sexualities are surely some of our most personal psychic concerns to the point that most counsellors and psychotherapists have made their claim to these as their territory or expertise. It would be true to say that most of us feel certain emotions and these are considered as naturally given, as though emerging from some deep recess within the body. Anger, sadness, depression, guilt, happiness and jealousy are just some of the 'natural' emotions that we experience and talk about in therapy, or that help therapists 'tune in' to the situations their clients describe. But should we make so many assumptions about feelings and emotions? Are they 'natural'? And how is it that the body simply 'knows' what emotion to manufacture at a given time? And if we as therapists denote our own sexuality as lesbian or bisexual or heterosexual or gay or queer, how will this impact on the way we formulate the meanings of emotion that our clients present in a session? And the emotions we label as our response?

In this chapter I use queer theory to explore emotions and sexualities because it provides an alternative framework to modern conventional models established, challenges the use of binary configurations and complicates identity. It provides us with a 'queer slant' (Beemyn and Eliason 1996:165) on self, identity and subjectivity. I will introduce findings from my own work that show emotions cannot be taken for granted as natural, thereby suggesting we queer ideas about emotion as well as sex, sexuality and gender. First I will introduce a fictional client, Lulu, who represents the various discourses that exist around sex, gender and sexuality, how these impact on everyday social, sexual and emotional life and are then presented within therapy. Second, I will address the role of emotion as heterosex convention and as a regulatory system, followed by the impact of my own research for therapy before suggesting a queer reading of Lulu's dilemma.

Lulu – straight, lesbian, bisexual or queer?

As an example of a client presentation, let us ponder on Lulu, a fictional client who presents herself to me and is struggling to make sense of who she is and who she is becoming.

Lulu, a white, able-bodied, middle-aged woman in her mid-forties, has entered counselling for the first time. She says that if anyone looks at her life, in all intents and purposes, she should be happily settled down by now. Her children have left home and she and her husband should be planning for their future. But this is not the case and her changing circumstances have brought her into therapy. After waiting for what seems a lifetime, Lulu has recently decided she must come out to her husband, children and family about the woman she has been intimate with for several months and friends with for several years. She says she loves this woman, and they have made plans to live together. She says they aren't to be thought of as lesbians, although they do share sexual feelings for each other. She says she loves this woman a great deal and wants to share her life with her before it's too late. She has come to counselling to discuss these and other issues that have rocked her normal, yet discontented life. She sighs as she says she is bound to meet with disapproval. At times she is upset and hesitant while telling the story. She looks down, saying she feels guilty for wanting her own happiness, feels terrible about loving someone else as her husband is such a good man, and is confused that she feels this strongly towards another person – especially a woman. She is concerned that, beyond the ridicule and sympathy, those she loves will consider her selfish and will ultimately reject her and say she is stupid for the 'mistake' she has made. She wants to know how she should act and what she should do. Is it really 'disgusting' to love another woman in 'that' way and should she stop right now and come to her senses? She says she feels so desperately confused and unsure about the future and what it holds for her or those she loves. She wants to be accepted for who she is – but who she is may not be accepted.

In a small way, this is a fraction of a story about 'coming out' brought into counselling and providing an insight into working with this particular client. It is not an unusual narrative and acts to inform counsellors about potential 'issues' when working with clients who shift sexual 'identity' from hetero to non-heterosexual. It incorporates some of the behavioural, cognitive and affective changes that may take place in relation to social and sexual worlds, and it means that therapists have an ideal framework from which to start the work of therapy. Lulu, the therapist may decide, is struggling with her sexuality and is feeling confused and anxious in the face of flux and change. She may be experiencing shame and fear because of her new-found feelings towards another woman. Could she be suffering the torments of internalised homophobia? Would this explain why she refuses to use the word lesbian in the description of her feelings towards her new relationship? Is she really bisexual? How will she address these changes with her husband and what will the fracturing of that relationship mean for her and her family structure? These are some of the areas that would possibly be explored between Lulu and her therapist.

At one level, Lulu's narrative may be seen as the product of modernity[1] issuing a set of meanings where the 'grand narratives' of gender, sex and sexuality are proclaimed to describe Lulu's personal feelings and emotion world[2] (Plummer 2001:214). In fact, Lulu's sexuality, gender and sex are predominantly understood as biologically driven, representative of modernity's essentialist rhetoric. In the case formulation of Lulu we will witness the 'twin processes' of modernity (Plummer 1992:13) at play in the form of chaos and potential change versus scientific classification and rationality. First of all, Lulu is seen to be experiencing chaos, change, possibility and flux to her identity, as it is divorced from heterosexuality. Her presentation of 'self' and therefore her sexuality and emotions will be open to classification, logic, rationality and bureaucracy instigated via an 'expert' represented by the therapist. As we read Lulu's story, we contextualise Lulu as a set of meanings that are taken from the 'grand narratives' of modernity. These prioritise binary systems and will help her to compose a narrative of the self that is both coherent and helps build a 'self' identity that extols the 'project of rationality' as issued by modernity. She is 'middle aged', she is 'heterosexual', she is a 'woman', she is a 'mother', she is 'white', she is 'able-bodied'. All these (and more) act as social markers, overtly or covertly informing the therapist, who is in the role of expert, about Lulu's position within social and sexual life, contextualising the 'type' of life she is constructing for her self and giving clues that Lulu fits into certain categories of social meaning, e.g. marriage has a socio-cultural function, it incorporates a division of labour and has a certain meaning within heterosexual society. In Lulu's narrative we can witness the binary, linear, rational heterosexual life that is now in a state of flux and change as it moves further and further away from fixed meanings denoting heterosexuality, bringing about fear and confusion at the possibility of transition to non-heterosexuality. The therapist's own knowledge and information will play a major part in contextualising Lulu, because the therapist will be listening to her story and will be trying to find out how Lulu is coping and how she is feeling as her emotion world begins to shift and change from heterosexual to non-heterosexual. However, I suggest that emotion, in line with the agenda of modernity, is presented as a binary system in relation to gender and sexuality and therefore the way Lulu is constructed emotionally will be limited by the narratives the therapist may choose from to frame an understanding of Lulu. How Lulu's emotionality is described reflects more about the cultural meanings of emotion, how these meanings are negotiated and how they are used to construct emotion worlds for particular populations – in this case non-heterosexual populations.

Ultimately, Lulu's story can be seen as the product of a conventional, binaried and regulated system, in contrast to new understandings of sex, sexuality and gender that are now emerging and are dwelling within a late modern[3] or postmodern[4] period. These incorporate 'queer' perspectives that are challenging the meta narratives of modernity (as we witness in this book) and the binarisms that exist within these. Lulu may be seen as presenting issues that the therapist may have little or no knowledge about because his/her own narratives (from training, texts etc.) are set within a modern, rather than late modern, perspective. In fact, Lulu's presentation is highly complex and reflects the positioning of both Lulu and her therapist within systems of knowledge. Queer theory provides a radical challenge that may be used to deconstruct Lulu's presentation because it stops essentialist thinking and challenges the way individuals are compartmentalized. It raises questions of identity, disputing the idea that individuals have a fixed identity, and therefore it is ideal for questioning Lulu's story because it 'questions the use of socially assigned categories based in the division between those who share some habit or lifestyle and those who do not' (Wikipedia 2006). In the following section I show why the shift from heterosexuality to non-heterosexuality that underpins Lulu's presentation, marks more than a shift in sexual identity. In fact, it articulates the very heart of modernity that has produced a heterosexualising of emotion.

The heterosexualisation of emotion

Background

The meanings of hetero and homo sexualities in relation to emotion have witnessed an intriguing, if somewhat disturbing trend whereby heterosexuality, taken as the bedrock of social and sexual relations, is used to structure and organise the knowledge or understanding of an individual (Richardson 1996a:3) even at the level of emotion, and regardless of the sexuality of that person. Emotional conduct and meaning becomes embedded within the hegemony of heterosexuality so that once emotion is heterosexualised and 'naturalised', it is used as a way of ordering the body. On the face of it, and particularly within the psy disciplines, emotion has mainly been considered as an intrinsic property of the individual – even where cognition is seen to influence certain emotions. Within psychology and counselling, theories of emotion date back to the end of the nineteeth century. These include the 'classical' theories of James (1890) and Watson (1931) leading to theories based on motivation, arousal and/or physiology. Later the behavioural and psychoanalytic theories emerged and also view named emotions as physiological products. It is within the cognitive theories that we have the most influential suggestions of emotion as integrated with meaning systems, as shown in Schachter and Singer's (1962) cognitive/physiological view of emotion where emotion states are determined by cognitive factors. More recently, social psychologists in the field of emotion and gender have extended research into emotion by considering the role of language, context and meaning (Fischer 2000).

Within sociological and anthropological studies,[5] emotions are considered to be social products. Studies by Kemper (1978) and Averill (1982) suggest a sociological analysis where emotions are considered through social relations and socialization. Particularly influential are the symbolic interactionist ideas such as those by Shott (1979) and Hochschild (1979, 1983) who take 'emotion' to mean the actor's cognitive labelling of what is being experienced physiologically. This has led to numerous sociological views about what exactly constitutes emotion and a move towards the idea that an emotion is socially constituted. For example pride and jealousy have no definite biological substrate and are 'socially, culturally and historically variable' (Williams 2001:45). Crawford, Kippax, Onyx, Gault and Benton (1992) point out that it is highly unlikely there are physiological correlates for each and every named emotion (they suggest there are at least 550 words and concepts for emotion), while many emotions have similar physiological correlates (Barbalet 2002), and some people describe the same emotion 'as having different phenomenological physiological sensations' (Crawford, Kippax, Onyx, Gault and Benton 1992:36). Crossley (2001:42) also remarks that emotion words are contextually defined, shown in the way people have a similar physiological response despite the variation to the context in which they are situated. For example, in certain contexts, the feeling of 'butterflies in the stomach' may be explained as 'love' while in another context as 'anxiety'. In effect, context shapes the meanings we assign to the bodily feeling states we then label as emotion. Thus, emotion words may be used to regulate the body in given social and sexual contexts.

The regulation of emotion and sexuality

The way we act and react to people, places or events is under intense self-surveillance most of the time, usually starting with how we 'feel' towards self, others and the world in general. For example, 'I feel angry about losing my job' or 'I love my partner' shows that we live in a social world that is constantly helping us negotiate our feelings and emotions. We have little choice but to connect the human body to the social body or 'in here to out there', through language where the vocabulary of feelings, used to describe inner experience, is matched to a socially organised 'dictionary of emotion' (Hochschild 1998:6). In this way, emotion words are rehearsed so frequently that they eventually appear as 'essentialised' ingredients of the social actor and are considered to be 'natural' products and expressions of the body rather than the product of socialisation.

It is through these means that emotion was used as part of what Elias[6] (2000: x) refers to as the 'civilising process', a socio-historical progression, beginning with the Middle Ages, 'whereby external restraints on behaviour are replaced by internal, moral regulation' (Marshall 1994:145). It culminates in what Elias refers to as a much deeper 'psychical process' of civilisation over many centuries where the meaning of behaviour and feeling slowly changes and the social, emotional and sexual conduct of men and women is gradually transformed into a civilized (and at times de-civilized through controlled behaviour[7]) manner paving the way for control over the body. In effect, emotions act as the mirror of society, reflecting the way social meanings are embodied through language, movement and gestures.

Heterosexuality is the product of such a rehearsal and emotion is central to its overall configuration. In fact, heterosexuality was only 'invented' (Katz 1996)[8] as a specific form of sexual conduct and identity once it had been designated, through various codes and rules, how boys and girls, men and women should behave, think and feel in relation to each other. The word 'heterosexual' like the word 'homosexual', is simply a scientific adjective, historically and socially immature (less than 150 years old in fact), and part of modernity's quest for order and rationality over the chaotic and irrational body. Both terms only surfaced in the latter part of the nineteenth century[9] (Katz 1996:52) when sexual acts and desires were seen to constitute 'identity' (Somerville 1996:241). Since then, heterosexuality has been organised, institutionalized and made more or less 'obligatory' (Rubin 1975 in

Katz 1996:133). It perpetuates because it provides a 'logic' that means it is continually socially produced and institutionalized (Dunne 1997:16). It is sustained at the macro and micro levels 'through our everyday sexual and social practices' where 'most of the population "do" heterosexuality every day without reflecting critically on that doing' (Jackson 1999:180). From magazines to all forms of media, TV, computer games, from soap operas to schooling, we may witness how heterosexuality remains influential in the construction of sex and meanings of sexuality through the various discourses it produces and reproduces (Braun, Gavey and McPhillips 2003). Once this is in place, we are then persuaded to believe that meanings about sex, sexuality and gender are 'real' binary systems (for example, we have the binarisms: masculine/feminine; boy/girl; homosexual/heterosexual), which, as Butler (1990) says, act merely as 'regulatory fictions' presenting dichotomous readings of sex, gender and sexuality that operate to maintain heterosexuality.

Shifting meanings

The very thought of stepping away from a given identity (as a man, woman, feminine, masculine, straight, etc.) can be terrifying for most people because emotion is inextricably linked to mental robustness denoting 'stability' and 'authenticity', represented primarily through the heterosexual body (Richardson 1996b). Within this representation, emotion plays a vital role because it is used to construct binary meanings that define an authentic and 'true' heterosexual masculinity and femininity that underpin meanings of psychosocial and heterosexualised gender differences[10] assigned into and onto the body and then reified as 'real' difference (Seidman 1992:123/124). Within this formation, heterosexual women have been understood as feminine with a subjectivity that is considered to be 'nurturing', 'caring', and 'irrational'. A woman is expected to show feminine traits whereby she 'cries easily', is 'very subjective' and 'very emotional' (Brownmiller 1984 in Lupton 1998:106/107). In comparison, heterosexual men are considered to display a subjectivity that has been emphasised through being 'blunter', 'rougher' and rational with masculine traits of being 'very direct', very logical' and 'never cries' (Brownmiller 1984 in Lupton 1998:107). According to Butler (1990:32), such meanings in relation to gender 'congeal' over time, appearing 'natural' because it is repeatedly being performed within a highly regulatory framework. Regulatory practices and social norms help provide a 'coherence' and 'continuity' of the person and are unlikely to be given up easily as they position the person within social structures and society. In fact, if persons do not offer 'gendered norms of cultural intelligibility' then they are likely to be deemed 'developmental failures' and their identity called into question (Butler 1990:17). In effect, unless each (heterosexualised) gender displays the appropriate (heterosexualised) emotions, they are chastised as somehow 'unnatural'.

Gendered and sexualised meanings of the body have led to those who want to shift meanings of sexual conduct from heterosexual to lesbian or gay male being made aware, through heterosexually organised and medicalized discourses (as Hegarty, Chapter Nine, points out, lesbians and gay men were excluded from conducting research) that in shifting meanings they are moving from a psychologically stable to an unstable construction of self. Emotion becomes central to the construction of a heterosexualised binary system to describe social, sexual and gender identities. Emotions and feeling have been used to regulate identity and play a central role in definitions of the self as unchanging, and as a fixed entity in relation to sex and sexuality, throughout the period of modernity. This is shown in the way we seem determined to make sure that our mental health is linked to who we share sexual feelings towards and how we express this through sexual conduct. Regardless of how unreasonable this appears to be – in the sense that it means we must never, ever, share any sexual feelings or sexual conduct with anyone of the same sex or gender – most people adhere to this rule through a process of extreme fear. I remember teaching counselling psychologists at Masters level who were seriously shocked by being asked what made them think they were the gender or sexuality they had always assumed they were 'born' with. What was also interesting was how they explained their feelings of 'being' a woman, or a man, or 'being' heterosexual and how frightened they were to think they could possibly experience feelings that were dissimilar – indicating the emotions they described were more socially enforced than naturally given.

The end result is that emotions are spread across the fictionalised sexualities and genders, reading as though they were entirely located and fixed within the body. In this discourse, it makes sense that when people do not fit the expected gendered and sexualised categories, they are defined through negative emotion words and narratives. For example, those who are non-heterosexual have been defined as 'pathological' (Herek 1984), while homosexuals were categorised through emotion words such as 'disgrace', 'shame', 'danger', 'guilt', 'anxiety' (Weeks 1986) with additional narratives that suggested they exhibited a 'weak moral fibre' were 'emotionally unstable' (Coyle and Kitzinger 2003) or 'mentally ill' (Herek 1984). For example, in the construction of a lesbian identity, lesbians are described as 'mannish',[11] they are 'masculinised' (they have too much testosterone) are 'quasi-men', with 'telltale signs' where, according to researchers who wish to be taken seriously, hearing and finger length are similar to heterosexual men! (McFadden and Pasanen 1998; Birke 2002:65).[12] Meanwhile, gay men are constructed as 'artistic' and 'sensitive' with a 'wavelike emotional temperament' (Carpenter 1908[2003]) and are defined as 'effeminate' (Birke 2002:65) in their comparison to heterosexual women. Beyond the pathos, this is incredibly unsophisticated, allowing heterosexuality to shape meanings of emotion, as well as gender, sex and sexuality simply by inverting heterosexualised meanings and assigning them onto and into the non-heterosexual body. It is this act of duplicity, this heterosexualisation of emotion, particularly embedded within the ideologies of modernity, that has been used to successfully malign the populations of those 'other-than' heterosexual over the past 150 years. In this way an identity of emotion is explicitly constructed for all those described as 'developmental failures', who go on to implicitly negotiate this in everyday life. As Weeks (1986:97) remarks, the social and subjective meanings attributed to 'homosexuality' by heterosexuals as well as lesbians and gay men are 'culturally specific' where 'emotions are differently structured according to different social forms and pressures'. Emotions are nothing more than regulatory fictions, offering signs to say how the sexualised and gendered body should feel and/or express feelings. However, these fictions have been made real, have been formed into truths about subjectivity and are used to separate one population from another – as befits the project of modernity. The next section highlights the role of therapy, a project embedded within modernity and a system that has also contributed to the regulation of the body through the use of emotion and feeling.

Therapy as a regulatory system of emotion

The rise of therapeutic ideologies and their location within the civilising process has taken prominent position within western discourses of the self, and in particular the sexual self, over the past hundred years. Therapeutic organisations have expanded to such a degree that they now 'influence and arguably dominate the public's system of meaning', thus shaping the predominantly heterosexualised 'cultural imagination' (Furedi 2004:17/1). Frank Furedi, in his book *Therapy Culture* (2004), talks about the increasing use of 'emotional scripts' and the growth of a 'therapeutic vocabulary' spreading throughout the pages of newspapers and magazines so that by now, most people have heard of 'self-esteem', 'anxiety', 'trauma' and 'stress'. At a personal, encounter and cultural level, the language of therapy (e.g. psychoanalytic statements such as 'you're being defensive', 'you're projecting' or cognitive behavioural therapy with homework projects and its focus on changing the way the person thinks) has become particularly influential, transported into everyday life, and entering the wider culture through television, magazines, books etc. Such ideologies – psychoanalytic, humanistic, behavioural, cognitive, transpersonal – mark the ways in which society and notions of the individual share a mutual reflexivity, with the emerging subjectivity under intense scrutiny from both the individual and society. It seems to me that most therapists operate with a similar degree of observation, checking out their therapeutic ideology to see that it is 'working' and introducing a therapeutic script to the client that leaves them both embedded within a particular discourse of modernity. If we begin to deconstruct the meanings of these discourses then we are reminded that emotions are words with 'powerful stories' that provide points of personal and collective significance (Fee 2000:75). For example, emotion words such as 'depression', 'anxiety', 'abuse' now circulate within our given culture and provide an individual with a set monologue but also provide an explanation for the variety of cultural and functional meanings attributed to emotion.[13] Similarily, emotion words have been used to describe non-heterosexual populations within therapeutic encounters.

As we saw in the previous section, the non-heterosexual body, in particular but not exclusively lesbian and gay male, has been marked through numerous emotion words. The question asked is where do therapists gather their information? How do they assess the emotions of non-heterosexual clients? How do therapists choose emotion words for their LGBT clients? It is certainly not something addressed in training because, as my own research (Moon 1994, 2002) with highly qualified lesbian, gay, bisexual, transgender (LGBT) and heterosexual therapists shows, none had received more than a few hours of training in LGBT issues (usually under the heading of sexual orientation but focusing on lesbians and gay men) on their courses, all admitted their knowledge was drawn from limited sources (their clients, friends, magazines, newspapers and television) and all admitted they were disappointed by their lack of knowledge about contemporary accounts of sex, sexuality and gender (refer also to Butler and Byrne's findings in Chapter Seven). Basically, without a more contemporary and psychosocial approach, therapists were really struggling to understand sex, sexuality and gender. Even where therapists said they did have an understanding, it was always framed through psychological knowledge and no therapist had any understanding of queer theory. A small section of this research is presented below to highlight how therapists subordinate the positioning of non-heterosexuals within society by using emotion and how they configure emotion in order that they may use it to fix an identity of emotion onto their clients.

Constructing emotion worlds

So far, I have argued that modernity privileges 'natural' binary systems and that emotion may also be considered as such a system, as evidenced within the therapeutic context. This section shows how sexuality and emotion have been regulated within therapy to the point of constructing emotion worlds for non-heterosexual clients. Between 1999 and 2000 (Moon 2002) I carried out an in-depth study of questionnaires and transcripts from 30 semi-structured interviews with fully qualified counsellors from the British Association for Counselling and Psychotherapy (BACP), Chartered

Counselling Psychologists from the British Psychological Society (BPS) and psychotherapists fully registered with the United Kingdom Council for Psychotherapy (UKCP). Seventeen were heterosexual and 13 were lesbian, gay male, bisexual and transgender. They ranged across a number of popular therapeutic modalities including: Cognitive Behavioural Therapy (CBT), psychodynamic, Transactional Analysis (TA), Gestalt, psychosynthesis, behavioural, systemic, feminist, and family therapy. They frequently worked in more than one model. All but one respondent included in the final 30 defined as 'white – UK'. All were aged between 30 and 65 years with a mode range of 51–55 and were able-bodied.

To begin with, my own research found a disjuncture between emotions and feelings. My own view is that emotions are words, shaped through cultural meanings to reflect society's overriding need for rationality and categorisation of the body, while feelings reflect the living, breathing, material body and their meanings are negotiated within the interaction either with self (reflexively) or other. In effect, although we do 'feel' at a visceral level (although we can also refer to feeling without really being aware of whether or not the body is feeling anything in particular e.g. 'I feel that you understand . . .' or 'It feels to me . . .'), feeling, of itself, is ineffable, indefinable and cannot be described without meaningful language, and language is symbolic of interaction. The body, because it is corporeal, has no meaning other than that bestowed upon it through language and language is a social product shaped according to the context people find themselves in.

How does this operate within the therapeutic arena?

In therapy we share, or try to share 'feelings', and they become defined by emotion words. Even where people struggle to say how they 'feel' then we work with that person to try and identify feelings 'in relation to' self, other, and the world in general or ask them to name emotions they are unable to 'feel'. Most clients talk about the way they 'feel' in relation to numerous issues including their self, their partners, their social world etc., and they name their feelings as emotion words such as depression, or fear, or upset or any number of common words. The way emotion is assigned to feelings indicates two points. First, we understand our cultural definitions of emotion and how they are used to fix the body within socially organised meanings. Second, we understand how to apply these meanings to the living, feeling body within a given social and/or sexual context.

What the research found: competing discourses of emotion and feeling frames

In the research I conducted, all therapists were asked to recall lesbian or gay clients they had worked with and to give examples of the discourses that emerged from the session in relation to their lesbian and gay clients' feelings and emotions. Therapists' responses were analysed and two significant findings emerged. First, in relation to comments on how they thought their lesbian and gay clients 'felt' emotionally in the sessions and second in relation to comments naming how they 'felt' working with lesbian and gay clients.

In the analysis I noticed that the pattern of responses differed between heterosexual therapists in comparison to lesbian and gay therapists. The most commonly used emotion words and concepts assigned to lesbian and gay male clients by heterosexual counsellors described lesbians and gay men as 'feeling': frightened, angry, aggressive, difficult, venomous, rageful, afraid (of heterosexual relationships), misogynistic, sick, guilty and shameful. Alongside, heterosexual therapists said they 'felt': anxious, incongruent, angry, afraid, scared, ignorant, rejected, frustrated and intolerant when working with lesbians and gay men.

In comparison, lesbian and gay counsellors presented narratives where emotion was organised differently. The most commonly used emotion words assigned to lesbian and gay male clients by lesbian and gay male counsellors, described lesbians and gay men as 'feeling': assertive, proud, self-responsible, decisive, anarchic, demanding (perfection of themselves), isolated (because of sexuality), sussed, intimate, vulnerable, afraid (of openly stating their sexuality in public), survivors and open (sexually). Alongside, lesbian and gay therapists said they 'felt': open (to their clients), questioning, supportive, empowered, congruent, anxious (for their client), honest, empathetic, trusted, committed, focused, sad (when listening to experiences they could identify with) and respectful.

These emotion words and concepts were embedded within various narratives therapists shared with me during the interviews. It certainly did not seem to be the case that counsellors realised which emotion words they had chosen. During the analysis it became clear that the choice of emotion words and concepts differed immensely between the two populations of therapists where the obvious variable is the sexuality of the therapist. This links to the idea of competing discourses (Carr 1999) that give meaning to sexual identity. Here, personal narratives (in this case of the therapist) and interpersonal scripts (in this case between the therapist and client) about sexual identity are given meaning through 'cognitive scripts' made available from cultural and social discourses. In my research findings, the dichotomous presentation of emotion words and concepts between the two populations appears to reflect how these different populations engage with cultural discourses about sexuality. However, these findings also indicate that something far more important is also taking place – that the choice of emotion word is literally a way of constructing the body of the 'other' in relation to 'self'. Emotion is literally constructed and assigned onto and into the body according to social context – in this case, the sexuality of the sender and recipient. The choice of emotion word signifies the relation of the person choosing the word and their engagement to cultural discourses.

Additionally, this process of negotiation within the interaction leads to a further finding where it became apparent that therapists reflexively configured their own feelings as a response. In this sense, feelings are heavily dependent upon the assumptions we hold in relation to cultural and social meanings. If our overarching belief system or framework is heterosexual, then the assumptions we make about the world will be based on and configured through that 'framework of frameworks', heterosexuality. These assumptions (about age, sex, social class etc.) are socially expressed, socially shared, and meanings in relation to them are imposed onto and into the body of self and/or other through feelings by how we say we feel towards others based on our relationship to these assumptions about social factors. They structure feelings of the body so that it is aligned with social meanings. In effect, we frame feelings according to social meanings. Using 'feeling' authenticates the bodily response, and then we really do believe that our feelings indicate our 'real' relationship to people, places or events. In this way, therapists are interpreting their clients' feelings in relation to assumptions about sexuality and then configuring their own feelings as an 'authentic' response.

A queer stance towards emotion

Taking a queer stance towards emotion means challenging the prevalent view that emotion is a physiological response that determines the formation of subjectivity. In effect, emotions are regulatory fictions used to control subjectivity and they need to be scrutinised intensely. Queer theory makes it a goal to question binarisms. To challenge the binarisms that exist in relation to sexuality and gender we need to challenge the idea that fixed emotions are assigned to heterosexual and gender categories. Once these are interrogated and expanded to include all emotions for either sex, sexuality or gender, then notions of what constitutes masculinity or femininity, men or women must also be up for grabs as these categories would then be destabilised as emotions would be shown to no longer fix the body within set meanings and identities. Instead, we need to consider how social actors assign emotions onto and into the body through feelings. In my study, I looked at what takes place in the interaction between a lesbian, gay male, or heterosexual counsellor and their lesbian or gay male client, how emotions are structured according to the sexuality of those in the interaction and how this influences the choice of emotion words assigned to the body of the client via feelings. Basically, the idea that emotions are natural, ordered responses of the body is highly suspect. In fact, it seems more likely that emotions are socially produced and are used to let us know how we need to behave, think and feel within our given society. As my own research shows, emotions are far from rigid and fixed within the body. In fact they are words that are socially organised, highly flexible, incredibly malleable and are constantly in a state of flux and change depending on the social actors involved and the context in which they find themselves.

So, let us briefly return to Lulu. By now it is possible to see how easy it would be to assign any number of emotions onto Lulu depending on you as therapist, your sexuality and what you understand about sex, sexuality and gender. Lulu can be fixed inside any number of discourses, and as a therapist it is for you to decide how you will position your client, edit her life, textualise her future. She will act as a template for your work with other clients and how you consign her to your future will be influenced by how you understand sex, sexuality, gender and emotion. In effect, the issues presented by Lulu may be deconstructed according to the underlying epistemologies of the therapist. Therefore, it is the responsibility of therapists to make themselves aware of the discourses surrounding sex, sexuality, gender and emotion so that these may help the client configure an understanding of the self in relation to social life.

Notes

1 Giddens (1991:14) refers to modernity 'in a general sense' to include the processes of industrialisation, capitalism, the nation state, 'the regularised control of social relations across indefinite time-space distances' (p. 16), the 'disembedding of social institutions', the introduction of temporal order, the psychological security of individuals and groups and the introduction of 'abstract systems'. Abstract systems are ways of disembedding social relations, and one way of doing this is through 'expert systems' represented by therapists who are considered to have a technical knowledge that is independent of the practitioners and clients that make use of the system. For example, counsellors refer to a therapeutic system that relies on trust and reflexivity – both aspects of the conditions of modernity rather than emanating only from somewhere deep within the self.

2 I want to thank Ken Plummer for the term 'emotion world' that I refer to in this chapter. An emotion world exists at a social level and organises what we commonly refer to as emotion. Emotion worlds may be constructed differently depending upon cultural values, rules and scenarios. They are the sum total of culturally shaped emotion words and concepts and designate how we are to respond emotionally at the cultural level. It is suggested in this paper that as heterosexuality is dominant, then this predominantly shapes emotion worlds.

3 Some authors suggest that we are in a period of late modernity, characterised by phenomena that mark the rapid change in social life while others suggest this is the beginnings of post-modernity.

4 Post-modernity is contrasted to modernity and is a state that advanced industrial countries are said to have reached. The social structure is said to be 'more fragmented', and the individual's personal identity is being fragmented over the life course (Abercrombie, Hill and Turne 1994).

5 Deborah Lupton (1998), Simon Williams (2001) and Jack Barbalet (2002) provide excellent overviews of emotion within sociological studies. Abu-Lughod and Lutz (1990) provide more anthropological and ethnographic accounts of emotion within given cultures.

6 Norbert Elias (1897–1990) wanted to understand the 'process of civilization'. His works focus on understanding the way emotion is used within society and the ways in which individuals are born into 'figurations of social inter-dependencies' that have evolved over time and reflect 'changing social and political structures of particular epochs' (Newton1998:62). See *The Civilizing Process* (Elias 1999) Volumes 1 and 2, where Elias focuses on how codes of emotional display are constructed sociohistorically.

7 Williams (2001:23) refers to the controlled 'decontrol' of emotion. For example, in sport and leisure where there is a demand to control the body while at the same time expressing emotions.

8 Jonathan Katz (1996) has written extensively about the 'invention' of hetero-sexuality and maps out the conception of heterosexuality and how it has become a dominant force since it was first named less than 150 years ago.

9 The terms are credited to Karl Maria Kertbeny in 1868 with homosexuality referred to in 1869 and heterosexuality in 1880 according to Katz (1996:53/54). Also, as Kertbeny is not in the bibliography section in Katz's book, it is better to read Note 51 for Chapter Three on p. 215.

10 Deborah Lupton (1998:105–36) in Chapter Four of her book talks at length about heterosexual emotional women and unemotional men. Interestingly, when she begins to refer to emotional men and the emergence of the 'more sensitive' feminised heterosexual male, there is little reference to gay men. This seems interesting considering that gay men have been constructed as 'feminine' and seems to employ the idea that heterosexual men may be heterosexually feminized rather than simply represent an emotional aspect of 'maleness' as exhibited by gay men, which would mean heterosexual and gay men are categorised within the category 'men' rather than artificially separated. Simon Williams (2001) in Chapter ix of his book falls into the same gender/sexuality/emotion trap.

11 Nikki Sullivan (2003:12) shows how the sexologists of the late twentieth century were troubled by the equation of lesbians to heterosexual men because if lesbians were likened to heterosexual men, then it would also be true that lesbian intellect matched that of heterosexual men rather than subordinated heterosexual women. To get round this, sexologists constructed a theory whereby the lesbian brain was depicted as 'similar to or sharing characteristics with "a non-white or lower-class masculine brain"' (Gibson 1998).

12 Birke (2002:65/66) quotes studies that found hearing tasks were found to be different between heterosexual women and lesbians, while lesbians have first and third finger length ratios that are more similar to heterosexual men.

13 According to social constructionists, the social overrules the biological. From this perspective, emotions are culturally and socially organised. Harré (1986, 1991) suggests that emotions as such do not actually 'exist' independently and are simply ways of acting and feeling emotionally. They refer to what people *do* rather than what people *are*.

References

Abercrombie, N., Hill, S. and Turner, B.S. (1994) *The Penguin Dictionary of Sociology*. London: Penguin Books.

Abu-Lughod, L. and Lutz, C. (1990) *Language and the Politics of Emotion*. Cambridge: Cambridge University Press.

Averill, J.R. (1982) *Anger and Aggression: An Essay on Emotion*. New York: Springer.

Barbalet, J. (2002) (ed.) *Emotions and Sociology*. Oxford: Blackwell Publishing.

Beemyn, B. and Eliason, M. (1996) (eds) *Queer Studies: A Lesbian, Gay, Bisexual and Transgender Anthology*. New York: New York University Press, pp. 163–8.

Birke, L. (2002) Unusual fingers: scientific studies of sexual orientation. In D. Richardson and S. Seidman (eds), *The Handbook of Lesbian and Gay Studies*. London: Sage.

Braun, V., Gavey, N., and McPhillips, K. (2003) The 'fair deal'? Unpacking accounts of 'reciprocity' in heterosex. *Sexualities*, **6**, 237–61.

Brownmiller, S. (1984) Femininity. In D. Lupton (ed.), *The Emotional Self* (1996). London: Sage, pp. 105–36.

Butler, J. (1990) *Gender Trouble: Feminism and the Subversion of Identity*. London: Routledge.

Carpenter, E. (2003[1908]) in N. Sullivan (ed.), *A Critical Introduction to Queer Theory*. Edinburgh: University Press.

Carr, C.L. (1999) Cognitive scripting and sexual identification: essentialism, anarchism, and constructionism. *Symbolic Interaction*, **22**, 1–24.

Coyle, A. and Kitzinger, C. (2003) (eds) *Lesbian and Gay Psychology: New Perspectives*. British Psychological Society: Blackwell.

Crawford, J., Kippax, S., Onyx, J., Gault, U. and Benton, P. (1992) *Emotion and Gender: Constructing Meaning from Memory*. London: Sage.

Crossley, N. (2001) *The Social Body: Habit, Identity, Desire*. London: Sage.

Dunne, G. (1997) *Lesbian Lifestyles: Women's Work and the Politics of Sexuality*. London: Macmillan Press.

Elias, N. (1994) *The Civilizing Process: Sociogenetic and Psychogenetic Investigation* [Trans. E. Jephcott] in E. Dunning, J. Goudsblom and S. Mennell (eds) (2000). Oxford: Blackwell.

Fee, D. (2000) *Pathology and the Postmodern*. London: Sage.

Fischer, A.H. (2000) *Gender and Emotion: Social Psychological Perspectives*. Cambridge: Cambridge University Press.

Furedi, F. (2004) *Therapy Culture: Cultivating Vulnerability in an Uncertain Age*. London: Routledge.

Gibson, M. (1998) The masculine degenerate: American doctors' portrayal of the lesbian intellect, 1880–1949. In N. Sullivan (ed.), *A Critical Introduction to Queer Theory*. Edinburgh: Edinburgh University Press, pp. 13–14.

Giddens, A. (1991) *Modernity and Self Identity: Self and Society in the Late Modern Age*. Cambridge: Polity Press.

Harré, R. (1986) (ed.) *The Social Construction of Emotion*. Oxford: Blackwell.

Harré, R. (1991) *Physical Being: A Theory for a Corporeal Psychology*. Oxford: Blackwell.

Herek, G.M. (1984) Attitudes towards lesbians and gay men: a factor analytic study. *Journal of Homosexuality*, **10**, 39–51.

Hochschild, A.R. (1979) Emotion work, feeling rules and social structure. *American Journal of Sociology*, **85**, 551–75.

Hochschild, A.R. (1983) *The Managed Heart: The Commercialisation of Human Feeling*. Berkeley: University of California Press.

Hochschild, A.R. (1998) Sociology of emotion as a way of seeing. In G. Bendelow and S.J. Williams (eds), *Emotions in Social Life: Critical Themes and Contemporary Issues*. London: Routledge.

Jackson, S. (1999) *Heterosexuality in Question*. London: Sage.

James, W. (1890) *The Principles of Psychology*. New York: Dover.

Katz, J.N. (1996) *The Invention of Heterosexuality*. New York: Penguin.

Kemper, T.D. (1978) *A Social Interaction Theory of Emotions*. New York: Wiley.

Lupton, D. (1998) *The Emotional Self*. London: Sage.

McFadden, D. and Pasanen, E. (1998) Comparisons of the auditory systems of heterosexuals and homosexuals: click evoked otoacoustic emissions. *Proceedings of the National Academy of Sciences of the United States of America*, **95**, 2709–13.

Marshall, G. (1994) (ed.) *The Concise Oxford Dictionary of Sociology*. Oxford: Oxford University Press.

Moon, L.T. (1994) Counselling with lesbians and gay men. *Changes*, **12**, 277–83.

Moon, L.T. (2002) The heterosexualisation of emotion: a case study in counselling with lesbians, gay male, bisexual and transgender clients', unpublished PhD Thesis, University of Essex, UK.

Newton, T. (1998) The sociogenesis of emotion: a historical sociology? In S.J. Williams and G. Bendelow (eds), *Emotions in Social Life: Critical Themes and Contemporary Social Issues*. New York, London: Routledge, pp. 60–80.

Plummer, K. (1992) *Modern Homosexualities: Fragments of Lesbian and Gay Experience*. London: Routledge.

Plummer, K. (2001) *Documents of Life 2: An Invitation to Critical Humanism*. London: Sage.

Richardson, D. (1996a) Heterosexuality and social theory. In D. Richardson (ed.), *Theorising Heterosexuality*. Buckingham: Open University Press, pp. 1–20.

Richardson, D. (ed.) (1996b) *Theorising Heterosexuality*. Buckingham: Open University Press.

Rose, N. (1989) *Governing the Soul: The Shaping of the Private Self*. London: Routledge.

Rubin, G. (1975) Thinking sex: notes for a radical theory of the politics of sexuality. In J.N. Katz (ed.), *The Invention of Heterosexuality*. London: Penguin.

Schachter, S. and Singer, J.E. (1962) Cognitive, social and physiological determinants of emotional state. *Psychological Review*, **69**, 379–99.

Seidman, S. (1992) *Embattled Eros: Sexual Politics and Ethics in Contemporary America*. London: Routledge.

Shott, S. (1979) Emotion in social life: a symbolic interactionist analysis. *American Journal of Sociology*, **84**, 1317–34.

Somerville, S. (1996) Scientific racism and the intervention of the homosexual body. In B. Beemyn and M. Eliason (eds), *Queer Studies: A Lesbian, Gay, Bisexual and Transgender Anthology*. New York: New York University Press.

Sullivan, N. (2003) *A Critical Introduction to Queer Theory*. Edinburgh: Edinburgh University Press.

Watson, J. (1931) *Behaviourism*. London: Kegan Paul, Trench and Traubner.

Weeks, J. (1986) *Sex, Politics and Society: The Regulation of Sexuality since 1800*. London: Longman.

Wikipedia (2006) *Queer Theory*. [Online]. www.wikipedia.org/wiki/Queer_theory [accessed May 2007].

Williams, S.J. (2001) *Emotions and Social Theory*. London: Sage.

Chapter 5

Queer(y)ing intersex
Reflections on counselling people with intersex conditions[1]

Myra J. Hird

Why are transbodies forced to pronounce a discourse on themselves in a way that those of the people studying us are not? Why are [intersex] people forced to produce a binary sexed identity? . . . What kinds of categories of analysis would emerge if nontransgender anthropological bodies were forced to explicate themselves in terms of intersexuality, rather than the other way around? What kinds of new insightful, and productive categories of analysis are out there, lurking just beyond the naturalized construction in which we all customarily traffic?"

Valentine and Wilchins (1997:220–1)

Background

Intersex is an umbrella term, under which a variety of conditions are placed, including androgen insensitivity syndrome, progestin induced virilization, adrenal hyperplasia, Klinefelter syndrome and congenital adrenal hyperplasia (Meyer-Bahlburg 1994). Definitions of these conditions appear on the Intersex Society of North America website www.isna.org. Cheryl Chase (1998) estimates that one in every hundred births shows some morphological 'anomaly' that is observable enough in one in every 2000 births to initiate questions about a child's sex. Accounts differ as to the statistical frequency of intersexuality. Anne Fausto-Sterling (2000) suggests two per cent of live births, approximately 80,000 births per year, demonstrate some genital anomaly. Out of those, approximately 2,600 children a year are born with genitals that are not immediately recognisable as female or male. Milton Diamond (2000) estimates the incidence slightly lower, at 1.7 per cent of the population.

Medical practitioners uniformly agree about the need to provide counselling support for people with intersex conditions and their families. At the same time, however, clinical treatment of individuals with intersex conditions is uncommon, due in part to the low incidence of intersex and, in part, to a general failure to recognise clients with intersex conditions (Oppenheimer 1995:1191). Moreover, a minority of medical practitioners in

North America and Britain are reconsidering the current medical management, and the often heated debate about the appropriateness of surgery is
well documented in both medical and intersex support group literature
(Wilson and Reiner 1998; Creighton and Minto 2001a, 2001b). One issue to
surface in this exchange is the lack of therapeutic intervention provided for
people with intersex conditions and their families. Much evidence suggests
that most of the minimal therapy available is provided by the consulting
physician, rather than a specifically trained psychotherapist.

There are a number of issues that a client with an intersex condition
might want to explore in a clinical setting:

- the development of trauma from repeated invasive surgeries, medical
  examinations (children with intersex conditions are often the subject of
  medical teaching and are routinely repeatedly examined by groups of
  medical students) and the aftercare procedures (for instance, when
  surgically constructed vaginas require daily dilation with a prosthetic
  device which is usually administered by parents until the child is old
  enough to self-administer);
- the development of trauma from the surgical alterations themselves
  (loss of erotic sensation);
- difficulties with parental and familial relationships (parents are routinely advised to withhold all information from their children about the
  intersex condition);
- ambivalent feelings regarding gender identity;
- ambivalent feelings regarding sexual orientation;
- ambivalent feelings regarding intimate relationships;
- the parent's mourning for the loss of the fantasised perfect daughter
  or son.

The aim of this chapter is to argue for the utility of developing a clinical
approach to intersex based on psychoanalytic theory. By reviewing the
existing clinical literature on intersex, I want to suggest that therapeutic
emphasis tends to be placed on maintaining a stable gender identity, and
clinicians largely accept the designation of gender as defined by the medical
team's determination. I will suggest the preoccupation with defining the
individual's 'true' sex limits the degree to which individuals with intersex
conditions are encouraged to explore other issues. I will further suggest this
emphasis on stable gender identity is linked with a valuation of heterosexuality over homosexuality. The emphasis on maturation presumes that
gender identification which does not correspond to at-birth gender
designation, and desire which is not opposite-gender directed, necessarily
reflects developmental issues. There is consistent concern in the medical
literature that an unstable gender identity will precipitate homosexual desire
(see Zucker and Bradley 1995; Zucker, Bradley, Oliver, Blake, Fleming and

Hood 1996; Slijper, Drop, Molenaar and Keizer-Schrama 1998). I hope to persuasively argue that Freudian psychoanalytic theory offers a cogent theoretical and clinical approach to intersex and its contiguous issues such as gender identity, intimate relationships, family relationships and sexual identity.

Clinical approaches to intersex

This section reviews the few studies currently published on the clinical work with individuals with intersex conditions, with a particular view to distilling their approach to gender identity and sexual desire. I am particularly keen to establish how such a focus on gender identity might influence treatment parameters. I will argue that approaches focused on gender and sexuality as immutable and stable 'internal characteristics' miss a valuable opportunity to work with individuals to explore alternate ways of interpreting their lived experiences which might alleviate distress and contribute to more positive familial and intimate relationships.

Traditional accounts

In 1931, William Fairbairn published an analysis of a person with an intersex condition (Fairbairn 1931) who had approached treatment with uncertainties about her gender identity.[2] Fairbairn is primarily concerned with establishing the client's 'true' sex, and so he sends her to three separate specialists for examination. Despite the fact that these three specialists provide contradictory assessments of the client's sex, Fairbairn nevertheless concludes that the client is 'really' a woman – determined in part because 'psychosexually . . . she certainly conveyed the impression of being a woman; and she had considerable attraction for heterosexual men' (p. 199). Fairbairn thus registers surprise that his client does not react negatively to the revelation that she does not have a vagina. There are indications throughout the analysis that the client might have wanted to explore her gender identity, but Fairbairn considers it unwise to disturb the original gender reassignment, or reveal to the client her physiologically intersexed condition. It appears to be of particular concern to Fairbairn that her gender identity as female be encouraged as this will provide a heterosexual framework for her sexual desire.

In *The Hermaphroditic Identity of Hermaphrodites*, Robert Stoller (1964) reports on the case of a person with an intersex condition who, in adulthood, reverses his medical reassignment as female to live as a man. This case adjoins an increasing number of reports of adolescent and adult intersexed individuals rejecting their assigned gender and choosing their own gender identity (Stoller 1964; Hurtig 1992; Meyer-Bahlburg 1994,

1998; Reiner 1999; Diamond 1998, 1999; Dittmann 1998; Slijper, Drop, Molenaar and Keizer-Schrama 1998; Hendricks 2000). Interestingly, Stoller analyses intersex as 'belong[ing] to an entity . . . not previously distinguished from other identity problems [that] . . . produces a different core gender identity and therefore a different life perspective' (p. 455). Nevertheless, Stoller reiterates the importance of medical and parental ascription of the 'proper' sex to intersex infants, in order to establish a core gender identity that is either female or male. Reporting on a case of a person with an intersex condition, Stoller determines that the client's gender-identity issues stem from parental doubt as to the correctness of the gender reassignment. There is no consideration that the trauma of surgery, or the intersexed body itself, might have initiated the client's gender identity questions.

In a later report, Stoller (1985) provides an analysis of Jack, an adolescent who was presumed female until virilization during adolescence prompted a medical workup that revealed male chromosomes and anatomy. Stoller recommends to the family that Jack change sex. Jack undergoes surgery, the family moves communities, and the young man's psychological, social and cognitive difficulties are resolved. Although Stoller rejects both biological and psychoanalytic explanations for Jack's gender identity issues, he surmises that Jack failed to establish a symbiotic relationship with his mother concomitant with his establishment of a strong identification with his father. Stoller concludes: 'the greatest mystery for me is the naturalness of Jack's masculinity. That, coupled with his lack of other neurotic problems, his successful and creative life, his openness, and his honesty is unexplained. Perhaps a psycho-analysis would uncover the roots of his normality, but one does not get to analyze such people' (p. 74).

In two successive studies Berg, Berg and Svensson (1982) and Berg and Berg (1983) report on the psychotherapeutic analysis of 33 men with hypospadias. Using interviews about childhood recollections and projective tests, Berg and Berg compare the group of men with hypospadias with a matched control group. Based on a psychoanalytic claim that body appearance (especially genital malformations) will affect an individual's gender identity, the researchers predict that men with hypospadias will have a less secure gender identity. Interestingly, while slightly more men with hypospadias were judged to have an uncertain male identity (19) compared to men with hypospadias who had a secure gender identity (15), 12 men in the control group were also judged to be uncertain in their gender identity (1983:158). Berg, Berg and Svensson do not find any greater tendency towards a homosexual object choice and conclude that 'the mere presence of a genital abnormality would . . . not be expected to disturb the development of *mature* object choice' (p. 162, my emphasis). In the second study, Berg, Berg and Svensson found that the men with hypospadias displayed slightly higher levels of neurotic constriction (1982:149).

The authors highlight the importance of the Oedipal phase in the formation of both gender identity and object choice, and they conclude that the realistic threat to the genitals faced by boys with hypospadias may cause higher levels of castration anxiety which in turn causes ego function impediments (p. 150). It is interesting to note that many children with hypospadias undergo repeated penile operations, often during the pre-Oedipal phase. The authors do not seem to consider that the trauma of repeated surgery during this phase might also affect ego functioning, particularly in terms of difficulties with trust and shame (Williams 2001a). Indeed, the authors use their results to recommend surgery during the pre-Oedipal phase. These 20-year-old studies have recently been followed up by Marc Mureau, Slijper, Slob and Verhulst (1997) who conclude that the men with hypospadias in their study did not have poorer psychosocial adjustment or greater behavioural or emotional problems than their age-matched comparison subjects (pp. 382, 385).

In 1985, Keppel and Osofsky reported on the intended treatment of a 14-year-old child with an intersex condition who had requested gender reassignment as male, again suggesting that the request for gender reassignment among people with intersex conditions is much higher than early reports suggest. The client is diagnosed with gender identity disorder, and 'her' desire for gender reassignment is attributed to a delay in surgery until 22 months of age coupled with parental doubts about the gender reassignment. The authors note that the outgoing and active child became withdrawn and shy after 'her' penis was removed and adamantly objected to oestrogen treatment in adolescence. Nevertheless, the authors refuse to entertain the adolescent's desire for gender reassignment; the young person refuses attempts to secure his gender identity as female and leaves treatment.

Agnès Oppenheimer (1995) provides a detailed case report of an analysis of a client with an intersex condition. Oppenheimer notes that while the psychoanalytic treatment of clients with intersex conditions is rare, the potential impact of such analyses is enormous, given the importance of sexual morphology for Freudian theories of gender identity and sexual development. Marielle is in her mid-thirties when she presents to Oppenheimer with persistent feelings of depression and difficulties with romantic attachments. In the course of therapy, Marielle reports having a dream in which she becomes a man but eventually accepts the gender identity that doctors assigned to her at birth as well as hormone treatment and a clitoral reduction. Marielle is one of five clients with intersex conditions that Oppenheimer has seen in therapy, and all five clients expressed doubts about their gender identity. Oppenheimer acknowledges the complex relationship between morphology and psyche within psychoanalytic theory. On the one hand, 'the drive is at the basis of destiny being determined by anatomy' (1995:1192). Freud notes that 'a certain degree of anatomical hermaphroditism occurs naturally' (1905c:142) which determines the primal bisexual disposition (Oppenheimer 1995:1192). On the other hand, Freud also argues 'the degree of physical hermaphroditism is to a great extent independent of the psychical hermaphroditism' (1920:210). Oppenheimer leans towards the latter interpretation – 'psychic factors predominate over biological determinism and anatomical characters' – but argues that in cases of biological ambiguity, an assignment of gender must nevertheless be made (1995:1192).

In a break with the previous analyses' predilection for reinforcing a stable gender identity and 'opposite' gender desire, Oppenheimer notes her own countertransference, prompted by her 'need for a basis in one sex' (1995:1201), which leads her to focus on therapeutic techniques that will help Marielle consolidate her female gender identity. Oppenheimer does suggest that her own difficulty in imagining Marielle as bisexual or sexless leads her, like Marielle's parents, to 'deny . . . her masculine part, which she was disavowing with my complicity' (1995:1195). Oppenheimer concludes the analysis by suggesting that 'psychic bisexuality, which is rooted in but independent of biology, accounts better for the development of the two sexes or the two genders' (1995:1202).

Hurray's (2001) treatment of a prenatally androgenized adolescent girl focuses on affirming 'her' gender reassignment as female, by encouraging the client to experiment with heterosexual sex. The client's reports of gender ambiguity are analysed as a wish formation, while her anatomical ambiguity is rejected as irrelevant to the analysis. In the same year, Rosario (2001) provides yet another report of a client with an intersex condition who, at the age of five, rejected his gender assignment as female, and at the age of ten is struggling with both positive and negative feelings about his masculinity, as he faces major reconstructive surgery. This is the second case report that draws on early Freudian psychoanalytic theory. Rosario suggests that assisting the client to identify as intersexed may prompt the client to reconsider the importance of reconstructive surgery (2001:8). Rosario's work counters the standard medical advice that telling a client that they have an intersexed condition will have a negative impact on the establishment and maintenance of a stable gender identity. Recent reports (Natarjan 1996; Creighton and Minto 2001a, 2001b) suggest that forthright disclosure actually enhances psychological functioning.

We may summarise these clinical accounts by focusing on presenting client concerns, clinical assumptions and therapeutic approaches. Common presenting concerns include:

- depression, anxiety, anger, neurosis and other affective symptoms;
- expressed ambivalence about gender identity and/or sexual orientation and/or sexuality. May include the desire for gender reassignment surgery;
- dissatisfaction with familial and intimate relationships, with particular concerns with trust issues.

As I have stated, it is often difficult to establish whether a client has an intersex condition (bear in mind that many intersex conditions go undiagnosed by medical practitioners and may only become visible when the individual, for instance, experiences fertility issues). As well as assessing the presenting problems, the client's history may reveal recollections of doctor and hospital visits and/or arguments with parents.

Since clinical assumptions direct therapeutic interventions, making these assumptions transparent is of vital importance. The traditional accounts cited above share a common concern with reinforcing societal norms about gender identity. The current medical treatment of children with intersex conditions adheres to the assumptions outlined by Kessler and McKenna (1978):

Environment is populated by two sexes and only two sexes.
People are morally dichotomised into sexes.

Adult member of society includes her/himself in this legitimate order, as a matter of rights.

Bona fide members of society are essentially, originally, in the first place, always have been, and always will be, once and for all, in the final analysis, either 'male' or 'female'.

Some insignia are regarded as essential in identifying function (vagina, penis), while others like emotions are more transient, temporary, accidental etc.

Recognition as either female or male is made for new members not just at birth but to entire ancestry and to posterity.

Presence in environment of sexed objects has feature of 'natural matter of fact'. 'Naturalness' has constituent meaning of being right and correct.

If we examine population of sexed persons at one time, and then examine at a later date, no transfers will have occurred from one sex status to the other, except for those transfers that are ceremonially permitted.

Males have penises and females have vaginas.

'Normally sexed persons' must have *either* a penis *or* a vagina. Either nature makes the organ, or the organ is constructed as *something that should have been there all along*.

To these assumptions I add:

Stable gender identification is a prerequisite for engaging in mature relationships.

These assumptions direct clinical interventions towards correspondence between genitals and sex assignment: a clear and stable female or male identity; correspondence between gender identity and sexual identity (for instance, a man defines himself as either heterosexual or homosexual rather than pansexual or transsexual); encouraging the client to identify and comply with prior medical gender determination and treatment.

For instance, Slijper, Drop, Molenaar and Keizer-Schrama (1998) argue that the major aim of the psychotherapeutic intervention with children with intersex conditions is to get the children to accept their gender reassignment. The authors assume that 'it is beyond the capability of a child to develop an intersex identity' (p. 142). The relationship between dimorphic bodies and psychosocial functioning is assumed to be both clear and strong. In an editorial comment, Ian Aaronson, Director of Pediatric Urology at the Medical University of South Carolina, writes, 'we live in an age of increasing respect for minority rights. However, to advocate nonintervention in intersex infants until they are old enough to make up their own minds about what gender they want to be signifies a return to the "dark ages" of intersex management, which has given rise to a host of *psychological cripples*' (Aaronson 1999:119; my emphasis).

The expression of gender ambiguity, desire to undergo gender reassignment or the resolute refusal of adults to undergo (further) surgical and hormonal intervention are often interpreted as problems of maturational development. Subjectivity is understood within a heteronormative framework, and this leads to both a narrow focus on genitals and an even more narrow view of how genitals should be experienced and used. For instance, Janine Chasseguet-Smirgel emphasises that one of the key forms of perversion is the denial of 'differences between the sexes' (1984:2). Otto Kernberg believes that 'infants establish a core gender identity that is male or female from the very start' (1995:48) as a prerequisite to the later development of mature relationships. Indeed, Kernberg argues that 'mature sexual love' is achieved in part through the 'integration of . . . representations of self into a consolidated self concept' (1995:34).

As the reports of therapeutic interventions indicate, success (defined by the terms of reference above) is limited, and therapy is often terminated by the clients themselves. I believe therapy is well placed to be more successful, not in terms of convincing individuals to adhere to societal norms governing gender and sexuality, but in terms of successfully negotiating feelings of self-worth, trust and relationships with others. To this end, I turn to an alternate therapeutic approach, first considering the theoretical framework then its clinical application.

Alternate approaches – harnessing Freudian psychoanalytic theory

Although never the subject of its own monograph, Freud makes constant reference to the subject of identification and the origin of selfhood. In *Totem and Taboo* (1913) Freud explicates the origin of culture and society whose authority governs behaviour. As Diana Fuss (1995) points out, key characteristics emerge concerning the character of identification. First, the son's eventual identification with his father is *ambivalent*: he hates his father for the power he wields, at the same time that he loves and admires him for this authority. Second, identification involves *violence*: the son kills and eats his father. Extrapolating from the myth we find the love object itself is not incorporated in its entirety, as the unconscious selects those elements that resonate most with the ego, so a certain degree of object 'mutilation' is necessary as the ego takes from the object its autonomous identity. Third, the ritual meal serves to reinvoke and undergird the original identification, underscoring the temporality and fragility of all identifications.

Published in 1917, *Mourning and Melancholia* draws an association between the loss of a loved one and the symbolic loss of connection the infant experiences when it becomes an autonomous subject. When a loved object dies, the ego is required to completely give up its libidinal attachment to this object. This is experienced as so traumatic that the ego temporarily attempts to retain the attachment by denying the reality of the loss. The reality principle eventually renders this attempt unsustainable, and bit by bit the ego surrenders to the knowledge that the loss is permanent. Incorporation is largely accomplished at an unconscious level. Mourning involves a certain degree of resistance as 'people never willingly abandon a libidinal position' (1917:154). The incorporation never fully replaces the love object, so the trauma of loss cannot be fully extirpated. The experience of direct object cathexis differs from that of the pleasure experienced from identification in that the real object is inaccessible for identification, and the interpretation, or memory trace, as it were, of the object by the ego must suffice. Absolute replacement is impossible and mourning accounts for the trauma of this limited assimilation. From the ego's perspective, there is no moral value attached to the object of love and desire; that is, there are no 'right' or 'wrong' identifications. Finally, the motivating force of the ego towards stability effects a colonising persistence.

Key aspects of Freud's discussion of the psychical processes of mourning might be taken up in our exploration of the origin of gender. Freud spoke alternatively of our inherent 'bisexuality' and 'polymorphous perversity', to emphasise our original undifferentiated identification and desire (1905a:280).[3] Further, Freud's analysis repeatedly emphasises that the undifferentiated infant enjoys a myriad of diffuse pleasures that the subject learns to restrict according to societal censure. Melanie Klein acknowledges that 'we know little about the structure of the early ego . . . the early ego largely lacks cohesion, and a tendency towards integration alternates with a tendency towards disintegration, a falling into bits' (Mitchell 1986:179; Goldner 1991; Brennan 1993; Benjamin 1994, 1996; Chodorow 1995; Layton 1998). This 'unfathomable' area, eager to experience pleasure in all of its polymorphous possibility, resists any attempts by the ego to narrow its sources. Klein was particularly aware of the anxiety, frustration and sense of loss incurred with the process of identification. She states 'at a very early age children become acquainted with reality through the deprivations which it imposes on them. They try to defend themselves against it by repudiating it' (Mitchell 1986:59). One sign of the 'achievement' of subjectivity is the child's demonstration of the 'ability to sustain real deprivations' (p. 59). Klein says further that the ego's 'attempts to save the loved object, to repair and restore it, attempts which in the state of depression are coupled with despair . . . are determining factors for all sublimations and the whole of . . . ego develop-ment' (p. 124). Freud was cognizant that the ego's struggle with the resistance of pleasures was unresolvable. In *Analysis Terminable and Interminable* (1937), he notes, 'a permanent settlement of an instinctual demand does not happen. The demand does not disappear. It is tamed' (p. 326).

All subjectivities that confine the expression of identification (and desire), which would include both femininity and masculinity, thus constitute compromises. To the extent that this 'inner world' is 'created through the denial of the "other"', this counts as pain' and is mourned (1937:146). Jacqueline Rose insightfully identifies the process of unconscious resistance to the closure of gender identity. She states:

> The unconscious constantly reveals the 'failure' of identity. Because there is no continuity of psychic life, so there is no stability of sexual identity, no position for women (or for men) which is ever simply achieved. Nor does psycho-analysis see such 'failure' as a special-case inability or an individual deviancy from the norm. 'Failure' is not a moment to be regretted in a process of adaptation, or development into normality . . . 'failure' is something endlessly repeated and relived moment by moment throughout our individual histories . . . there is a resistance to identity at the very heart of psychic life.
>
> (1986:90–1)

Freud even refers to intersexuality directly, to argue that primal poly-morphous perversity is biologically determined. He writes, 'For it appears that a certain degree of anatomical hermaphroditism occurs naturally' (1905c:142), and 'the psychic character traits depend to a greater or lesser extent on their somatic counterparts' (1905b:220).

Freud's radical theory of the ambivalence of identification sits uncomfortably beside the now more familiar aspects of psychoanalytic theory – the Oedipal complex and derogation of female sexuality – found in *The Interpretation of Dreams* (1999), *Three Essays on the Theory of Sexuality* (1905c) and *Beyond the Pleasure Principle* (1961). How are these conflicting claims balanced? Partial explanation resides in Freud's own theoretical shifts as he develops a meta-psychology of the death drive and the Oedipal constellation, both of which introduce a temporality that will structure psychic processes and indeed the human condition itself. This is a movement from pleasures to bodies (Simon and Blass 1991).

The conflicting claims are also explained by Freud's attempt to evacuate psychoanalytic theory from a gnawing internal paradox. The radical social constructionist position from which Freud initiates his theory of polymorphous perversity juxtaposed against an overwhelmingly compromised heteronormative culture obliges Freud to introduce a criterion exempt from cultural relativism. This criterion is sexual reproduction. While Freud is clear that sexual activity is end-pleasure oriented and that there is no biological or evolutionary preference for reproduction, the shift in focus to this 'end-result' effects a powerful association between sexual development and maturity. As Freud states, 'every pathological disorder of sexual life is rightly to be regarded as an inhibition in development' (1905c:208). So, Jerome Neu points out, 'perverse sexuality is, ultimately, infantile sexuality' (1991:185). Infantile sexuality might then be afforded free reign of nongenital forms of pleasure, as perversions are now associated with 'regressed' and/or 'fixated' pleasures rather than mature genital love. As Neu succinctly observes, 'In practice . . . Freud collapses the individual's experienced concern for genital pleasure together with the biological function of reproduction, so that the development and maturation criterion for perversion reduces to the question of the suitability of a particular activity for reproduction . . . An ideal of maturation that gives a central role to that function [reproduction] makes all earlier sexuality necessarily perverse. The infant's multiple sources of sexual pleasure make it polymorphously perverse' (1991:187).

So what does this look like in practice? Or, how might these insights be utilised in the counselling context? Nina Williams (2001b) offers by far the most promising analysis in terms of an acknowledgement of early Freudian psychoanalytic theory. The report concerns the case of Kristin, who initiates therapy because of lifelong depression. Over the course of therapy, Williams and Kristin work at uncovering the reasons for Kristin's therapy: childhood recollections of doctor's appointments and arguments with her parents, dreams and the medication that Kristin has been instructed to take because of a 'hormonal imbalance' eventually lead to discussions about Kristin's body and her feelings of insecurity and doubt that there is 'something wrong with her' (2001b:6). As Kristin becomes able to recall more memories of her medical treatment, the therapy focuses on Kristin's feelings of helplessness against medical and parental authority, trauma from the treatment, and her deepening conviction that her femininity was due more to the medication than a clearly 'female' body (2001b:7). Through dream analysis, Williams recounts a pivotal experience in Kristin's life, that of being terribly shocked when she trusted her parents and doctors: 'She described the doctor's appointment . . . when she was subjected to a pelvic examination by a male doctor who said only "I need to see your scars". Later she talked about her having "male hormones", and it was at this moment, as a shy twelve-year-old alone on an examination table, that Kristin began to replace her belief that doctors had damaged her with a worry that there had been something wrong with her to begin with' (2001b:7–8).

As well as focusing on the many, conflicting feelings that Kristin is dealing with in therapy, Williams acknowledges her own preoccupation with determining whether Kristin has an intersex condition and her reluctance to talk to Kristin about this. Williams's honesty in dealing with this preoccupation 'finally allows Kristin to express her anger at me [Williams] for wanting to know the cause of her condition rather than focusing on the trauma of its treatment' (2001b:10).

Conclusion

I suspect it is the case that since counsellors do not usually encounter individuals who suspect or know they have an intersex condition, questions about the relationship between gender morphology and gender identity remain a case for abstract theory rather than actual individual analysis. When individuals with intersex conditions are encountered in a therapeutic setting, it is largely left to the counsellor to use their own conceptions of gender identity (Williams 2001b). In this way, other issues such as trauma, trust, shame, anger and helplessness as well as the potential to explore feelings of gender ambiguity are eclipsed by the concern for stable gender identity.

While it has traditionally been assumed that psychopathology found among the intersex population is caused by the trauma of growing up with a gender anomaly, coupled with parental doubts about the appropriateness of the gender identity assignment of their child, there is growing evidence to suggest this may not be the only possible explanation. First, it is not at all clear that individuals who grow up with genital anomalies experience psychological or developmental issues. John Money reported in his 1951 PhD dissertation that the ten intersex individuals he interviewed, who had had no surgery or hormone treatment, showed no evidence of neurotic psychopathology (Colapinto 2000). This report is significant, as Money went on to forge the standard medical protocol for intersex infants, involving repeated surgical procedures and hormone treatment. Morgan Holmes reports that of 'seventy case studies of adolescents and adults who grew up with visibly anomalous genitalia . . . only one . . . was an individual deemed potentially psychotic, and the potential illness was connected to a psychotic parent and not the sexual ambiguity' (1995:5). Joan Hampson and John Hampson write: 'the surprise is that so many ambiguous-looking clients were able, appearance notwithstanding, to grow up and achieve a rating of psychologically healthy, or perhaps only mildly unhealthy' (Fausto-Sterling 2000:95). Recall that Berg and Berg's studies found an almost equal number of men in the control group had questions about their gender identity, as did the men with hypospadias. As Bruce Wilson and William Reiner note, 'it is increasingly clear that children can come to recognize their differing gender identity from their infancy-assigned identity without major psychological collapse or psychiatric illness' (1998:365).

And while there are a plethora of studies that hypothesise the risks to gender-reassigned boys of developing gender identity issues from not being able to urinate in a standing position, win at urination contests, or experiencing embarrassment when changing in public locker rooms (Mureau, Slijper, Slob and Verhulst 1997), researchers are only beginning to consider the risks of developing psychosocial problems from the trauma of the surgery, medical and parental withholding of information, and the effect of the parents' own trauma on their child. To give just one example, the surgical creation of a vagina in children who are gender reassigned as female requires a lifelong programme of vaginal dilation with prosthetic devices up to three or four times per day. As Sallie Foley and George Morley write, '. . . the paediatrician must depend more on parental involvement with vaginal dilation. If the client is too young to understand dilation, then reactions of anxiety, anger, depression and fear can become associated with the parents' attempt to continue this mechanical therapy. Thus, ironically, procedures designed to promote adjustment and normalcy for these clients can instead result in psychosexual problems' (1992:74).[4] Tamara Alexander (1997) argues that this type of medical management constitutes childhood sexual abuse, and Suzanne Kessler provides compelling evidence that parents expected to dilate their children's surgically constructed vaginas feel the same (1998:58–64).

Moreover, it is not at all clear that gender reassignment 'works' in the sense of providing a clear basis for a child's sense of gender identity. It is now increasingly clear that 'the primacy of early sex assignment, potential sexual function, fertility, and the cosmetic appearance of reconstructed genitalia as clinical decision-making rubrics might appear to be an assumption, not a deduction' (Reiner 1999:364). The number of people with intersex conditions seeking gender reassignment in adolescence and adulthood, and the growing politicisation of people with intersex conditions against surgery that they consider to be both nonconsensual and cosmetic, *at the very least* suggest that intersex gender identity is more complicated than current management protocols allow. Nor is it clear that gender reassignment increases the likelihood of 'opposite' gender desire, although this is clearly a major concern for clinicians (Lev-Ran 1974; Dittmann, Kappes and Kappes 1992; Hurtig 1992; Slijper, Van der Kamp, Brandenburg, de Muinck Keizer-Schrama, Drop and Molenaar 1992; Zucker and Bradley 1995; Zucker, Bradley, Oliver, Blake, Fleming and Hood 1996; Bradley, Oliver, Chernick and Zucker 1998). A number of studies suggest that sexuality is a much more fluid and complex phenomena. Moreover, many gender-reassigned individuals identify as lesbian or gay (Creighton and Minto 2001b).

I have argued that possibilities for alternate readings of psychoanalytic theory may indeed present a space to challenge the uncritical acceptance of sexual difference and maturational goals. Broadly, we must ask what bodies with intersex conditions might mean for a theory of the body and psyche generally. Rather than providing a theory of intersex gender identity and desire, the more powerful analysis seeks to contemplate a theory of gender identity and desire from a position of intersex, of morphological diversity.

Next, we need to increase awareness about intersex so that counsellors will more easily identify the presenting issues associated with these conditions. The counsellor's aim need not be primarily concerned to reinforce medical decisions about gender reassignment. Indeed, focusing on the 'intersexed body' may only solidify the child as a symbol of disorder and monstrosity (Oudshoorn 1994; Williams 2001a, 2001b; Hird 2002). It may also decrease the likelihood that individuals with intersex conditions will seek counselling, if the perception is that their feelings of gender ambiguity will not be heard. Correspondingly, rather than primarily attempting to establish the individual's 'true' gender and encouraging them to accept the gender that has been assigned to them, counsellors need not reject the notion of gender ambiguity. Indeed, 'in many intersex situations, one can argue that it is not a sign of mental disorder but a sign of appropriate awareness when a client has questions about his/her gender' (Berg and Berg 1983:28). I am not suggesting that the aim of counselling be to encourage individuals to identify as intersexed. It is clear that most individuals with intersex conditions identify as either women or men. This identity need not, however, preclude the exploration of feelings of gender ambiguity.

Notes

1 This chapter is based on a longer version that appeared as Considerations for a psychoanalytic theory of gender identity and sexual desire, *Signs: A Journal of*

Women in Culture and Society, **28**, 1067–92, 2003 published by the University of Chicago Press. © 2003 by the University of Chicago. All rights reserved.

2 The bulk of reports on intersex emanate from the US, although Fairbairn's work is in Britain, Berg and Berg's work is in Sweden and Oppenheimer's analysis took place in France. It is too early to speculate as to whether the movement towards the recognition of gender identity ambivalence seen in the most recent American cases (Williams and Rosario) extends beyond a US context.

3 Freud also speaks of our 'psychical hermaphroditism' (1920:210) and our 'predisposition towards bisexuality' (1905a:136).

4 The Frank procedure is a preferred treatment because it does not require surgery. However, dilation of 20 to 30 minutes, three to four times a day, is still required, with the major aim of creating a vagina that can 'receive' a penis. Foley and Morley's article is representative of the majority of medical articles that assume the major consideration will be 'normal' heterosexual relations and the desire to have children (see Randolph, Hung and Rathlev 1981).

References

Aaronson, I. (1999) When and how to screen? *Infectious Urology*, **12**, 113–19.

Alexander, T. (1997) *The medical management of intersexed children: an analogue for childhood sexual abuse*. [Online] www.Isna.org/library/analog.html [accessed May 2007].

Benjamin, J. (1994) The shadow of the other (subject): intersubjectivity and feminist theory. *Constellations*, **1**, 231–54.

Benjamin, J. (1996) In defense of gender ambiguity. *Gender and Psychoanalysis*, **1**, 27–43.

Berg, R. and Berg, G. (1983) Castration complex: evidence from men operated for hypospadias. *Acta Psychiatrica Scandinavica*, **68**, 143–53.

Berg, R., Berg, G. and Svensson, J. (1982) Penile malformation and mental health: a controlled psychiatric study of men operated for hypospadias in childhood. *Acta Psychiatrica Scandinavica*, **66**, 398–416.

Bradley, S., Oliver, G., Chernick, A. and Zucker, K. (1998) Experiment of nurture: ablatio penis at 2 months, sex reassignment at 7 months, and a psychosexual follow-up in young adulthood. *Pediatrics*, **102**, 1–5.

Brennan, T. (1993) *History after Lacan*. London: Routledge.

Butler, J. (1990) *Gender Trouble: Feminism and the Subversion of Identity*. London: Routledge.

Butler, J. (1993) *Bodies That Matter: On the Discursice Limits of Sex*. London: Routledge.

Chase, C. (1998) Hermaphrodites with attitude: mapping the emergence of intersex political information. *GLQ: A Journal of Gay and Lesbian Studies*, **4**, 189–212.

Chasseguet-Smirgel, J. (1984) *Creativity and Perversion*. London: Free Association Books.

Chodorow, N. (1995) Gender as a personal and cultural construction. *Signs*, **20**, 516–44.

Colapinto, J. (2000) *As Nature Made Him. The Boy Who Was Raised as a Girl*. London: Quartet Books.

Coventry, M. (2000) Making the cut. *Ms. Magazine*. [Online] www.msmagazine.com/oct00/makingthecut.html.

Creighton, S. and Minto, C. (2001a) Managing intersex. *British Medical Journal*, **323**, 1264–5.

Creighton, S. and Minto, C. (2001b) Objective cosmetic and anatomical outcomes at adolescence of feminizing surgery for ambiguous genitalia done in childhood. *Lancet*, **358**, 124–5.

Diamond, M. (1998) *Management of intersexuality: guidelines for dealing with individuals with ambiguous genitalia.* [Online] www.ukia.co.uk/diamond/diaguide. htm [accessed May 2007].

Diamond, M. (1999) Pediatric management of ambiguous and traumatized genitalia. *Journal of Urology*, **162**, 1021–8.

Diamond, M. (2000) *Some current views on management and therapeutic issues in children and adolescents with intersex conditions.* Presented at Atypical Gender Identity Development: Therapeutic Models, Philosophical and Ethical Issues Conference, Tavistock/Portman Clinics, London, 17–18 November 2000.

Dittmann, R. (1998) Ambiguous genitalia, gender-identity problems, and sex reassignment. *Journal of Sex and Marital Therapy*, **24**, 255–71.

Dittmann, R., Kappes, M. and Kappes, M. (1992) Sexual behavior in adolescent and adult females with congenital adrenal hyperplasia. *Psychoneuroendocrinology*, **17**, 153–70.

Fairbairn, W. (1931) Features in the analysis of a client with a physical genital abnormality. In W. Fairbairn (ed.), *Psychoanalytic Studies of the Personality*. London: Routledge, pp. 197–222.

Fausto-Sterling, A. (2000) *Sexing the Body: Gender Politics and the Construction of Sexuality*. New York: Basic Books.

Foley, S. and Morley, G. (1992) Care and counseling of the client with vaginal agenesis. *The Female Client*, **17**, 73–80.

Freud, S. (1905a) Fragment of an analysis of a case of hysteria. *Collected Papers*, vol. 3. [Trans. A. Strachey and J. Strachey] New York: Basic Books.

Freud, S. (1905b) My views on the part played by sexuality in the etiology of the neuroses. *Collected Papers*, vol. 1. [Trans. J. Riviere] New York: Basic Books.

Freud, S. (1905c) Three essays on the theory of female sexuality. *The Standard Edition of the Complete Psychological Works of Sigmund Freud*, vol. 7. [Trans. J. Strachey with A. Freud] London: Hogarth Press.

Freud, S. (1913) *Totem and Taboo*. London: Routledge and Kegan Paul.

Freud, S. (1917) Mourning and Melancholia. *Collected Papers*, vol. 4. [Trans. J. Riviere] New York: Basic Books.

Freud, S. (1920) The psychogenesis of a case of homosexuality in a woman. *Collected Papers*, vol. 2. [Trans. J. Riviere] New York: Basic Books.

Freud, S. (1937) Analysis terminable and interminable. *Collected Papers*, vol. 5. [Trans. J. Strachey] New York: Basic Books.

Freud, S. (1961) *Beyond the Pleasure Principle*. New York: W.W. Norton.

Freud, S. (1999) *The Interpretation of Dreams*. Oxford: Oxford University Press.

Fuss, D. (1995) *Identification Papers*. New York: Routledge.

Goldner, V. (1991) Toward a critical relational theory of gender. *Psychoanalytic Dialogues*, **1**, 249–72.

Hendricks, M. (2000) Into the hands of babes. *Johns Hopkins Magazine*, September. [Online] www.jhu.edu/~jhumag/0900web/babes.html [accessed May 2007].

Hird, M.J. (2002) Unidentified pleasures: gender identity and its failure. *Body and Society*, **8**, 39–54.

Holmes, M. (1995) *Queer cut bodies: intersexuality and homophobia in medical practice*. [Online] www.usc.edu/isd/archives/queerfrontiers/queer/papers/holmes.long [accessed May 2007].

Hurray, A. (2001) *A plea for a measure of uncertainty*. Anna Freud Lecture. New York Freudian Society, New York City.

Hurtig, A. (1992) The psychosocial effects of ambiguous genitalia. *Comprehensive Therapy*, **18**, 22–5.

Keppel, W. and Osofsky, H. (1985) A client with ambiguous genitalia and gender confusion. *Bulletin of the Menninger Clinic*, **49**, 584–95.

Kernberg, O. (1995) *Love Relations: Normality and Pathology*. New Haven, CT: Yale University Press.

Kessler, S. (1998) *Lessons from the Intersexed*. New Brunswick: Rutgers University Press.

Kessler, S. and McKenna, W. (1978) *Gender: An Ethnomethodological Approach*. Chicago: University of Chicago Press.

Layton, L. (1998) *Who's That Girl? Who's That Boy? Clinical Practice Meets Postmodern Gender Theory*. Northvale, NJ: Jason Aronson Inc.

Lev-Ran, A. (1974) Sexuality and educational levels of women with the late-treated adrenogenital syndrome. *Archives of Sexual Behavior*, **3**, 27–32.

Meyer-Bahlburg, H. (1994) Intersexuality and the diagnosis of gender identity disorder. *Archives of Sexual Behavior*, **23**, 21–40.

Meyer-Bahlburg, H. (1998) Gender assignment in intersexuality. *Journal of Psychology and Human Sexuality*, **10**, 1–21.

Mitchell, J. (1986) (ed.) *The Selected Melanie Klein*. London: Penguin.

Mureau, M., Slijper, F., Slob, K. and Verhulst, F. (1997) Psychosocial functioning of children, adolescents, and adults following hypospadias surgery: a comparative study. *Journal of Pediatric Psychology*, **22**, 371–87.

Natarajan, A. (1996) Medical ethics and truth-telling in the case of AIS. *Canadian Medical Association Journal*, **154**, 568–70.

Neu, J. (1991) *The Cambridge Companion to Freud*. Cambridge: Cambridge University Press.

Oppenheimer, A. (1995) Considerations on anatomical and psychic reality in relation to an intersexual client. *International Journal of Psycho-analysis*, **76**, 1191–204.

Oudshoorn, N. (1994) *Beyond the Natural Body: An Archaeology of Sex Hormones*. London: Routledge.

Randolph, J., Hung, W. and Rathlev, M. (1981) Clitoroplasty for females born with ambiguous genitalia: a long-term study of 37 clients. *Journal of Pediatric Surgery*, **16**, 882–7.

Reiner, W. (1999) Assignment of sex in neonates with ambiguous genitalia. *Current Opinion in Pediatrics*, **11**, 363–5.

Rosario, V. (2001) The boy with labia: intersexes and iatrogenic transsexualism. Lecture presented at Yale University.

Rose, J. (1986) *Sexuality in the Field of Vision*. London: Verso.

Simon, B. and Blass. R. (1991) The development and vicissitudes of Freud's ideas on the Oedipus Complex. In J. Neu (ed.), *The Cambridge Companion to Freud.* Cambridge: Cambridge University Press.

Slijper, F., Drop, S., Molenaar, J. and Keizer-Schrama, S. (1998) Long-term psychological evaluation of intersex children. *Archives of Sexual Behavior*, **27**, 1251–44.

Slijper, F., Van der Kamp, H., Brandenburg, H., de Muinck Keizer-Schrama, S., Drop, S. and Molenaar, S. (1992) Evaluation of psychosexual development of young women with congenital adrenal hyperplasia: a pilot study. *Journal of Sex Education and Therapy*, **18**, 200–7.

Stoller, R. (1964) The hermaphroditic identity of hermaphrodites. *Journal of Nervous and Mental Disorders*, **139**, 453–7.

Stoller, R. (1985) *Presentations of Gender.* New Haven, CT: Yale University Press.

Valentine, D. and Wilchins, R.A. (1997) One percent on the burn chart: gender, genitals, and hermaphrodites with attitude. *Social Text*, **52/53**, 215–22.

Williams, N. (2001a) Personal correspondence with author, October 7.

Williams, N. (2001b) *The imposition of gender: psychoanalytic encounters with genital atypicality.* Paper presented at the American Psychological Association Conference, San Francisco, August.

Wilson, B. and Reiner, W. (1998) Management of intersex: a shifting paradigm. *Journal of Clinical Ethics*, **9**, 360–9.

Zucker, K. and Bradley, S. (1995) *Gender Identity Disorder and Psychosexual Problems in Children and Adolescents.* London: Guilford Press.

Zucker, K., Bradley, S., Oliver, G., Blake, J., Fleming, S. and Hood, J. (1996) Psychosexual development of women with congenital adrenal hyperplasia. *Hormones and Behavior*, **30**, 300–18.

Chapter 6

Queer(y)ing gender and sexuality

Transpeople's lived experiences and intimate partnerships

Tam Sanger

As there are no tests for transgenderism, the ultimate evidence is the client's own experience.

Anderson (1998:222)

Introduction

Medical and psychological discourses have exerted a great deal of influence on theoretical understandings of trans, and concomitantly, on the frameworks available to counsellors working with transpeople. These discursive frameworks tend to reinforce the sex/gender binary and also reify heterosexuality as the 'norm' against which other sexual orientation identities should be measured (Green 1987, 1992; Money and Ehrhardt 1972). Green explicates, 'If sexual identity is seen to have three components: core identity ("I am male" or "I am female"), gender behavior (culturally "masculine" or "feminine"), and sexual orientation (heterosexual or homosexual), the transsexual is . . . atypical on all three' (1992:120).

Green's presumption here is that the typical configuration for a 'normal' individual is that of either a man who is culturally masculine and heterosexual, or a woman who is feminine and heterosexual and transpeople transgress these norms.[1]

There is no consideration of transpeople (or people in general even) as a diverse group who cover a broad spectrum of sex, gender and sexual configurations. This chapter suggests that it is time to move beyond conventional models of gender and sexuality that do not extend wide enough to encapsulate the myriad identities currently being articulated, and indeed lived out (Carroll, Gilroy and Ryan 2002; Raj 2002). Within the majority of current literature, understandings of trans lives are limited to those who identify as heterosexual and transsexual, thus erasing those others who inhabit spaces outside of this positioning. My aim in this chapter is to offer a perspective that challenges the limitations inherent in much literature and practice, in order to open up a space for those who are currently on the margins of societal and medico-psychological under-standing and acceptance.

Background

The history of trans has been one of medicalisation, pathologisation and stigma. 'Gender identity disorder' is listed as a mental health disorder in the fourth edition of the American Psychiatric Association's *Diagnostic and Statistical Manual* (*DSM-IV*) (1994:532–3), and transpeople have been pathologised in this publication since their inclusion under the previous term 'transsexualism' in 1980. Similarly, the Harry Benjamin International Gender Dysphoria Association (HBIGDA) is a group of individuals who are involved in providing medical care to transpeople and have come together to issue 'standards of care'[2] that are used by medical practitioners as guidelines. The existence of guidelines for treatment removes the auton-omy of medical professionals dealing with transpeople, who then cannot freely utilise their own judgement in relation to care pathways. Medical discourse on trans also tends to be dissociated from transpeople themselves, such that treatment is not generally influenced by patient input, and transpeople remain categorised in a way which does not accord with self-perception for many (Sanger 2006).

One result of this pathologisation and decreased autonomy is that trans-people are likely to need higher than average rates of counselling and therapy than non-trans individuals on average (Anderson 1998; Bockting, Knudson and Goldberg 2006). This is often because psychological assess-ment is a precondition for diagnosis as trans, as well as access to often-desired medical intervention (Carroll, Gilroy and Ryan 2002). On the other hand, it could be due to the negative effects of the marginalisation endured by transpeople within society (Califia 1997; Namaste 2000). Throughout this chapter I shall focus primarily on issues of diversity within the 'trans community', and also between partners of transpeople, who may or may not be perceived as part of this community. Counsellors need to be aware of the heterogeneity of trans experiences in order to offer appropriate assistance in each individual case presented to them.

Within counselling arenas emphasis tends to be placed on the issues transpeople face, with the experiences of their partners becoming subsumed or ignored. Transpeople's partners are often also in need of counselling services, as are other family members and friends, such that counselling practices should expand to include all those involved in transpeople's lives and affected by possible transitions (see Bockting, Knudson and Goldberg 2006). This could occur within family therapy services, through the training of counsellors and therapists in trans-specific issues. I shall illustrate the heterogeneity of trans experiences through consideration of a number of brief case examples, focusing on issues around intimate partnerships and the need to move beyond normative understandings of gender, sexuality, and intimate partnership formations.[3]

There are many debates surrounding the nomenclature of transpeople, and as such it is necessary for me to set out the definitions I intend to use. 'Transpeople' here refers to those whose gender identity does not equate to that assigned at birth, with 'transman' indicating an individual who was assigned the gender 'female' at birth but identifies as a male, and 'transwoman' referring to those who identify themselves as female despite early assignation as male. Other terms such as 'genderqueer' are used for those who do not identify within the gender binary. In terms of sexuality, terms such as 'bisexual,' 'pansexual,' 'asexual,' and 'queer' indicate a movement beyond the homosexual/heterosexual binary.

The instability of gender and sexuality

In contradistinction to the medical and psychological assumptions set out above, a differentiated group of transpeople has recently become more visible. Transpeople are further distinguished from one another when aspects of identity such as gender, sexuality, age, and intimate partnership status are considered. With this in mind, new meanings and counselling practices need to be established (e.g. Carroll, Gilroy and Ryan 2002). Devor states '[I]t is important to remember that, for many people, SOLD [sic] is not stable. SOIDs [sexual orientation identity] are, in part, built on a foundation of sex and gender identities. These are not static for most transsexual persons' (1994:8). Counselling and therapy for transpeople is often guided by medical and social notions of binary gender and sexuality, thus excluding those whose genders and/or sexualities are temporally variable or uncategorisable.

Trans has invited useful challenges to societal assumptions about the 'constitution' of gender (Hird 2000). One of the major issues to emanate from such analyses is the elision between gender identity and sexuality. Despite the inclusion of transpeople in groups focused on sexuality, as in the case of LGBT organisations, it is important to retain a sense that trans identities are based around gender, and that this is a separate, though related issue, to sexuality. It is necessary to move beyond perceiving transpeople as purely another 'sexual minority' who can be subsumed under existing models of 'gay' or sexuality-specific counselling.

In terms of sexuality, trans-related literature gives little acknowledgement that transpeople may also be bisexual, lesbian, gay, or identify with any other available sexuality marker, and that this sexuality may moreover be fluid throughout transpeople's lives. Trans is, as mentioned above, frequently conflated with sexuality, so that the sexuality of those who identify as trans, or are perceived as such by others, is presumed to be uniform. This uniformity is often reinforced by clinicians, counsellors and therapists, who tend to re-articulate generalistic ideas about transpeople that may not fit with the lived experiences of clients. An oft-encountered limitation of approaches to trans is the belief that '[C]lients may be male or female, hetero-, homo-, or bisexual' (Anderson 1998:223), when in fact many trans lives extend beyond such identifiers (Sanger 2006).

Decentring of genitalia

An important link between transpeople's gender and sexuality is explained by Devor, who states: '. . . people who suffer through a profound search for identity, especially when that identity is so entirely entangled in the contours of their sexual body parts, would feel intensely motivated to explore whatever sexual options they perceive as open to them' (1994:13).

As such, transpeople are likely to go through a process of exploring their attractions to others, with the result that sexual identifications may alter, remain the same, or become more or less stable over time. Sexuality, as shall be seen in the case studies examined here, is a central concern for transpeople and their partners. Similarly, individual sexual orientation identities are generally taken to depend on genitals and are presumed to be uncomplicatedly discernable if the gender identity of a partner is known, for those currently involved in an intimate partnership. For transpeople this cannot be taken to be the case, and as a result sexuality cannot be said to be stable over time in all cases.

Within intimate partnerships involving transpeople, genitals are often decentred as the most important indicator of gender, and thereby sexuality. The sexualities of transpeople and their partners sometimes fluctuate throughout the trans-identified partner's transition (or both partners' transitions, if both are trans-identified) and sexuality may be based on genitals, gender, or something else entirely. The basis of sexuality identification may also move between these factors.

Susan and Tim, despite being perceived as a heterosexual couple, do not identify as such. Susan sometimes categorises herself as bisexual, but also tries to move beyond an understanding of sexuality based upon binary gender, and will therefore often use terms such as pansexual and omnisexual. Tim prefers not to label his sexuality. He is a transman who has taken hormones and had his breasts removed, but is not interested in phalloplasty as he sees no point in changing his body, due to not seeing genitals as indicative of gender. Susan perceives gender as existing on a continuum and her attractions are not based on gender identity or genitals. Both Tim and Susan identify as polyamorous.[4] Tim has little interest in sex and argues that friendship and sexual relationships are not as distinct as they are generally understood to be. As friendships and intimate partnerships tend to be differentiated mainly through whether or not sex is involved, those who do not desire sexual interaction tend to find that such distinctions do not speak directly to their own experiences. Susan's father does not know about Tim's trans identity and perceives Tim and Susan as a heterosexual couple. They plan to adopt children if they decide to have any, even though either of them could in theory bear a child, as Tim stopped taking hormones some time ago.

The normative notions of sex and gender that underpin dominant counselling frameworks do not allow for non-normative sexualities, and as such need to be reconsidered by practitioners. Transpeople often cannot conceive of themselves within the dominant norms in society and therefore need to look elsewhere for answers to identity issues (Gagne, Tewksbury and McGaughey 1997:482).

As Devor has noted, '[A]lmost all published information about the sexuality of FTM TSs [female to male transsexuals] has either been from (auto)biographical or clinical sources' (1994:6). Another more recent space in which trans lives have been articulated is in the media, where the homogenisation and stereotyping apparent in clinical settings is often recreated. As such, it is important that therapists and counsellors are wary of becoming negatively influenced towards transpeople, through media representations as well as psycho-medical literatures.[5] Not all transpeople's ultimate goal is genital reassignment surgery, transpeople's sexualities and gender identities are diverse and often fluid, and there are people who identify as trans outside the binary gender system. Some recent sociological and queer theoretical insights into transpeople's experiences could pose a useful challenge to current normative expositions, which are more readily available to counsellors and therapists (e.g. Califia 1997; Hines 2006; Hird 2000, 2002; Namaste 2000; Prosser 1998; Sanger 2006). The following is a typical example of the way people present a challenge to taken-for-granted knowledge about trans lives.

Sam and Jo identify as genderqueer and 'in between genders' respectively. Their genders have altered over time and are not defined in any particular way. They married recently due to Jo needing to acquire UK residency. This involved having to be referred to by the genders on their birth certificates, which were 'opposite' to one another. Both found this very difficult, as they had tried so hard to escape the limits of the gender binary but had to return there for the purpose of the marriage. Sam, who prefers mixed gender pronouns, identifies his sexuality as queer but has used identities such as asexual and bisensual in the past. This reflects her lack of comfort with rigidly defined identity markers, as well as the shifts that have occurred in his attractions and desires. Jo identifies slightly more with the male than the female gender, and favours male pronouns, but prefers not to label his sexuality as he feels it is too complex to be encapsulated by a unitary label.

Limits of medical approaches within counselling and therapy

As discussed above, within a medico-psychological approach to trans, individuals are assumed to conform to the gender binary. However, this presumption limits trans to those who identify unproblematically with the so-called opposite sex to that assigned at birth. Transpeople who do not identify with either the male or the female gender are erased from view. Thus, those who are not included in the limited medical framework have difficulty gaining medical treatment. Marina and Greta's story exemplifies this situation:

Marina and Greta have been a couple for four years. Marina identifies as genderqueer and is interested in having her breasts surgically removed but has found that because she is not interested in the full medical route prescribed for transpeople, including hormones, getting a referral is difficult. She thinks it is important that the medical profession moves past the assumption that gender can only exist in binary form. Greta identifies herself as bisexual or queer, and female, and despite her acceptance of Marina's genderqueer identity, she is concerned about how she would be affected by Marina's breasts being removed. She is also unsure about the seeming inconsistencies between Marina's desire for breast removal and her interest in bearing a child. She knows that these positionings are almost unthinkable within the current medical framework and that Marina will probably have to have a child before breast removal rather than after, if she chooses to pursue both.

The labelling of trans as a mental illness through the inclusion of 'gender identity disorder' in *DSM-IV* (American Psychiatric Association 1994) has led to a situation in which transpeople are likely to either submit to this diagnosis or rebel against it, although some adhere to some aspects of medicalisation and not others. Classification of trans as a mental illness has thus led to rifts within the 'trans community', as no one really wishes to be pathologised, but this tends to be seen as the only way to gain access to any medical assistance, which may impact on some individuals' ultimate survival (see Butler 2004; Namaste 2000; Whittle 2002).

Implications for treatment

This section focuses on the ways in which the narratives of transpeople and their partners can inform counselling practice, particularly with respect to the centrality of the body, and issues that may arise in relation to transpeople's partnerships.

Presentation of the self

The confusion, for those who do not identify as trans, that often proceeds from transpeople's presentation of self is evident within clinical analyses, where statements such as the following are abundant, 'female-to-male transsexuals tend to form stable, long-term relationships with the same sex partner, (that is, a female) though both partners view this relationship as "heterosexual"' (Steiner and Bernstein 1981:178). Here, the transperson and his partner define their sexualities in relation to the genders they identify with, whereas clinically their relationship is considered to be same-sex, based on genital configurations. In this way transpeople and their partners may find their identifications subsumed by medical understandings, and this is something which counsellors must be aware of, rather than relying unquestioningly upon psycho-medical literatures.

Louise's story indicates the complexity that can emerge for transpeople with respect to the relationship between their gender identification and body morphology.

> Louise is a 23-year-old transwoman who has moved through a number of identificatory possibilities throughout her life. Formerly identifying as a 'gay boy', she then moved towards a bisexual identity, before assigning the transsexual label to herself. Eventually she felt most comfortable identifying as 90 per cent female and 10 per cent male, thus not adhering strictly to one or other side of the gender binary. In the past she presumed she would have genital reassignment surgery, as she thought this was the only possibility for her as a

transwoman. However, she met her transman boyfriend and realised that surgery was not necessary in order for her to have an intimate partnership. She has not pursued genital reassignment surgery and is now comfortable living as a 'woman' with a penis.

The body is of central importance to many transpeople and must be considered as such within counselling settings. While some transpeople argue that they require genital surgery in order to be able to carry on with their lives, others do not feel so strongly and may be influenced by the widespread assumption that all transpeople desire to alter their genitals. Counsellors must be aware of this pressure to conform to genital reassignment and the existence of other possibilities when working with trans clients. As George Brown has pointed out in relation to cross-dressers and their partners, '[P]apers were written from the perspective of a treating health-care professional sitting behind a desk talking to a self-identified patient. Information was then generalized to the population of cross-dressers and their spouses at large' (1998:353). This analysis of clinical understandings is also applicable to other trans-identified people who tend to be theorised as a homogeneous group without consideration of the narratives of a diversified sample. According to Brown, '[O]ne could also make the case that the existing literature was potentially damaging to these couples in its inappropriate generalizations and unsupported conclusions and did nothing to facilitate the process of communication and self-disclosure so vital to these relationships' (1998:354).

This is also true of transpeople as defined within this chapter for whom there is very little information on offer relating to intimate partnerships with that which *is* accessible postulating a particular way of being that often does not correlate with lived relations. As Gagne, Tewksbury and McGaughey point out, '[W]hile new identities are emergent, they are created within the constraints of current understandings' (1997:490). These constraints include the influence of normative psycho-medical approaches, as well as other societal norms, including those reified through the media.

Relationships with others

Trans-trans partnerships

Transpeople may form partnerships with one another, often finding these trans-trans relationships easier in terms of not having to explain trans in great detail, and as offering increased understanding of their lived experiences.

Belinda, Jenny and Lee all identify as trans and polyamorous. Jenny is in partnerships with Belinda, Lee and one other person (non-trans female), as well as having two tocotoxen ('too complicated to explain'). Belinda has been with Jenny for a few months and has one other partner (non-trans female) who she has been with for ten years. Lee has been in a relationship with Jenny for six years, and also has one other partner (transvestite male). Lee found that his interactions with the medical establishment involved a lack of understanding of polyamory, with psychologists and gender specialists referring to his second partner as his 'special friend' and refusing to recognise each of his partnerships as equally valid. Jenny has little interest in the sexual aspect of partnerships and finds that being poly is useful in this respect, as her partners can have sexual encounters with their other partners and thereby not have a problem with the lack of sex in their relationship with Jenny. Belinda found that she did not have to explain trans to Jenny as she also identified as such and had been through similar things such as taking hormones, making decisions about surgery, and encountering transphobia. Whereas there had been issues between her and her non-trans partner because of the questions Belinda's trans identity raised for their partnership. Lee stated that he is attracted to transpeople, and especially men or transwomen who wear skirts, linking this to a desire to problematise the gender binary.

The case study above indicates the complexities that may be encountered with respect to transpeople's intimate partnerships. Awareness that transpeople, like non-transpeople, are not a homogeneous group who engage in one particular type of partnership is central to moving beyond current limited frameworks.

Desiring transpeople

Just as two or more transpeople may be in a partnership together, there are those (trans and non-trans), like Lee above, who are specifically attracted to transpeople. The choice of a partner who identifies as trans is often seen, particularly within the psycho-medical model, to be a peculiarity, and reasons are sought for anyone choosing such a partnership (Blanchard and Collins 1993; Steiner and Bernstein 1981). Steiner and Bernstein, who have devoted an entire article to questioning the reasons for non-transwomen being in intimate partnerships with transmen, argue that choosing a transman as a partner – 'that is a "man without a penis"' – may be a safe compromise, perhaps a protection against further pregnancies or a defence against involvement with biological males with whom they have had unsatisfactory emotional experiences in the past' (1981:181).

Those with trans identified partners often argue that their relationship is intrinsically no different from any other. However, for many, attraction to transpeople signals the possibility of breaking free from societal constraints around gender and sexuality, rather than indicating a problematic desire.

> Alex and Lisa are no longer intimate partners. However, they both have very positive memories of their time together, particularly with respect to the fluidity of gender and sexuality encountered within the partnership. Alex identifies as genderqueer, while Lisa generally identifies as female, while endeavouring to problematise the gender binary by sometimes performing more of a boyish or androgynous identity. Sexually, Alex and Lisa would perform a variety of genders and sexualities, thus exploring the limits of these concepts and not restricting themselves to particular identity categorisations based around their bodies and genitals. Lisa was very encouraging of Alex's genderqueer identification, finding the movement beyond the gender binary to be exciting, as well as enabling in terms of her own gender and sexuality explorations.

Individuals such as Alex and Lisa offer a challenge to counselling practices that engage with trans partnerships as problematic, offering an alternative position from which to consider the issues therein. Counsellors should not expect all partners of transpeople to present with misgivings about their partner's identification as trans and would be better served adopting a more variegated stance, allowing for each individual case to emerge without preconceptions.

Public recognition

The ways in which others perceive the genders and sexualities of transpeople and their partners can be of central importance to the sense of self of each individual, although the particular issues vary from couple to couple.

> Jason and Eve both identified as females and lesbians in the past. Jason now identifies as a queer transman and Eve, though still identifying as a female, has shifted her sexual identity to queer in order to encompass her partnership with Jason. Eve is often mistaken for a man, such that she and Jason may be perceived as a gay male

couple if he is passing as male. At times when Jason has not passed they have been understood to be either a heterosexual or a lesbian couple, depending on how Eve is categorised. When Eve is perceived by others as a female and Jason as a male they are labelled heterosexual. The labels other people attach to Jason and Eve may vary widely but they are generally not perceived as a queer couple when each is understood as the gender they actually identify with. Eve finds being categorised as a heterosexual woman difficult, as she holds that heterosexual relationships are inherently unequal and she does not identify in any way with heterosexual women.

While Jason's trans identification is not directly a problem for him, instances of public recognition are central to his sense of self. As such, it is imperative that counsellors take on board the impact that others may have on a transperson's notion of their place within society. As is clear from Eve's story, it is also important to acknowledge that recognition as heterosexual can be a problem for those who have previously been recognised otherwise, with a trans partner's transition often leading to changes in both gender and sexuality identifications, or the perceptions of such by others.

Legal recognition

The recent passage into law of the Gender Recognition Act (Great Britain. Parliament 2004a) and the Civil Partnership Act (Great Britain. Parliament 2004b) have had a considerable impact on transpeople's lives and partnerships.[6] In terms of counselling, transpeople may present with issues relating to applications for gender recognition certificates, that allow for a change to the gender recorded on an individual's birth certificate, perhaps requiring evidence from a counsellor of having lived as the gender they identify with for a certain amount of time. These legal changes have not been received positively by all transpeople or their partners. Those who married in the gender assigned at birth are required to divorce before the trans-identified partner(s) may apply for a gender recognition certificate. Birth certificate alterations are also not of use to those who identify outside the gender binary, as the change can only be from female to male or vice versa.

Myfanwy and Judith were married for twenty-five years prior to Judith's transition. During Judith's transitional period, from male to female presentation, Myfanwy had problems dealing with the physical changes, such as beard removal, breast growth and vocal changes.

They almost got as far as divorce but decided against it in the end. Myfanwy came to understand her attraction to others as not based on gender – something she had considered but rejected when she was younger. She also discovered BDSM as an extremely important part of her sexual identity, coming to see potential partners' dominant sexualities as more relevant than their gender. Myfanwy and Judith now live in a triad with Keith, who joined their relationship five years ago. The Gender Recognition Act posits that for Judith to apply to change the gender on her birth certificate from male to female she and Myfanwy must divorce. The couple could gain a civil partnership, but Myfanwy feels they should not be made to divorce. She also argues that those in polyamorous partnerships should be able to marry multiple partners.

It is necessary for counsellors to be aware of the impact the Gender Recognition Act and Civil Partnership Act may have on both transpeople and their partnerships. Those couples, like Myfanwy and Judith, who have avoided divorce in the past and are now attempting to make important decisions about whether to remain married or apply for a gender recognition certificate may desire counselling to aid in this decision-making process.

Queer theoretical insights

Over time, a more fluid, postmodern conceptualisation of trans has superseded the arguably more traditional emphasis in psycho-medical and mainstream sociological studies. In such analyses, according to Myra Hird, social constructionist positions have been

> largely displaced by deeper explorations of the ontological status of key concepts such as gender, race, ethnicity, age and disability. Within gender and sexuality studies, sociologists seek to challenge the 'naturalness' of sex, gender and sexuality.

(2002:577–8)

Queer theory has moved beyond sociological debates in posing a challenge to normative heterosexuality and advocating a more fluid conceptualisation of gender and sexuality (Butler 1990; De Lauretis 1991; Seidman 1996). My analysis of trans counselling practices emanates in the main from a queer positioning, due to a desire to enable inclusion of all transpeople and recognition of those who are often overlooked or excluded due to not fitting in with dominant contemporary categorisations.

Not all transpeople are driven by a desire to conform to the other side of the gender binary, with increasing numbers of people problematising the confines of current understandings of gender and sexuality and attempting to carve out a space for themselves beyond restrictive binaries. Models of trans have moved from a 'transsexual model' to a 'transgender model' according to Dallas Denny (2004), mainly in the US but also increasingly within the UK, due to the impact of queer conceptualisations of gender and sexuality and the broader range of issues and positionalities considered within a queer framework.

For those who recognise that 'identity' is 'continually (and complexly) negotiated in today's gender/sexuality movements' (Broad 2002:261) and live their lives as such, medical determinations that involve a stable and easily-knowable identity are irreconcilable with lived experience. Many transpeople today are questioning the restrictions imposed upon genders and sexualities. As Broad recalls, '[R]ather than advocating for the right to change genders and be accepted, some transactivists reveled in the ideas of existing between and among both gender categories' (Broad 2002:254–5). Lack of conformity to the gender binary does not negate a wish to be accepted by others and society as a whole. However, as society is based so squarely on the gender binary, acceptance is less likely to be forthcoming, and assistance may be required in coming to terms with stigmatisation and marginalisation.

Conclusion: considerations for counsellors and therapists

The importance of therapists' and counsellors' input into trans lives is evidenced by research findings such as Gagne, Tewksbury and McGaughey where it has been stated that '[I]n addition to the facilitating function of support groups, many transgenderists reported that their public proclamations were in large part propelled by encouragement (or instructions) from a therapist' (1997:500). Thus, the influence of those who counsel transpeople may mean the difference between hiding their identity and proclaiming it to the world at large, and anywhere in between.

Important issues that may need to be considered when counselling transpeople or their partners include sexual identity and experience, body image, societal acceptance, hormonal intervention, surgery and its implications, transphobia and related violence, decisions about whether to 'come out' as transgendered, and support networks, both for those who are transgendered and for their partners. It is also important to remember, however, that transpeople are liable to have the same issues as anyone else in addition to anything specifically related to their trans identification.

As has been asserted above, it is paramount that counsellors be aware that not all transpeople want to fit into the dominant gender order, but that those who remove themselves from binary positionings may still feel the need for counselling as they are living in opposition to societal norms and risking intimidation and violence. As Gagne, Tewksbury and McGaughey have pointed out, '[T]hose who are willingly or unwittingly unconvincing in their gender presentations and interactions are subject to greater levels of emotional and physical abuse than are those who are able to pass' (1997:504). Counsellors must make it clear that transpeople do not need to conform to one way of being and will not be judged under the auspices of a medical understanding which only recognises the desire to move towards one end or the other of the gender binary. As Broad attests, '[W]hile there are many MTF/transwomen who are very clear about their desire for sex-reassignment-surgery (SRS), there are growing numbers of people who are advocating a vision of womanhood that might include a penis' (2002:257). There are transpeople moving beyond the confines of the gender binary, and concomitantly the homo/hetero sexual orientation binary, and a more open and thorough understanding of such lives is necessary within coun-selling practice (e.g. Carroll, Gilroy and Ryan 2002; Raj 2002).

It is incumbent upon counsellors to suspend any judgements based on social norms that they may hold and to allow for possibilities that expand the perceptions of gender, sex and sexuality currently in place. Barbara Anderson says of her own practice, 'because diagnoses can be tools of discrimination, I do my best not to use them. Descriptive statements about a particular individual are far more informative and useful than a formal category subsumed under a group of mental disorders' (1998:222).

Further, those counselling transpeople and their significant others need to be aware that '[G]oing public with a transgendered identity could be an intimidating experience, to say the least' (Gagne, Tewksbury and McGaughey 1997:495). It is also intimidating for those who are close to the transperson, be they supportive, unsupportive, or anywhere in between.

Transpeople suffer many pressures, within a society that often denies their full citizenship, and even existence. As such, it is imperative that counselling is one place in which they can feel accepted and understood. Anderson argues that '[C]ontributing to rapport in this particular popu-lation is the therapist's mastery of solid information about this condition and the ability to convey to the client a sense of comfort with the subject' (1998:223).

Many counsellors who specialise in the treatment of transpeople identify as trans themselves and are therefore likely to boast a greater knowledge of trans issues. However, it is equally necessary for trans-identified counsellors to retain awareness of the diversity that exists within the 'trans community', rather than assuming their own experiences may be generalised to all transpeople.

The case examples included in this chapter indicate the diversity that exists among transpeople and their partners. Each of the individuals considered would conceivably bring very different issues to a counselling situation, and counsellors working with transpeople and partners would therefore need to avail themselves of a wide and varied understanding of trans issues, as well as remaining open to further possibilities not considered in this short exposition. Less uniformity within counselling practice may enable transpeople to consider gender and sexuality options beyond those rendered possible by societal norms and values. Such a reconceptualisation would sit comfortably within the realm of queer theory and contemporary society's expanding potential.

Notes

1 However, only socially acceptable transgressions tend to be considered within clinical literature.
2 These can be found at www.hbigda.org/Documents2/socv6.pdf [accessed May 2007]. The most recent revision to the document was made in 1998.
3 These case studies originate from my PhD research and as such are used as a tool to offer a broader perspective on transpeople's experiences, rather than indicating cases that were considered within a counselling setting. As such, each individual may or may not have pursued counselling or therapy.
4 Polyamory refers to a preference for having more than one intimate partner.
5 Although, as Carroll, Gilroy and Ryan point out, there have also been some more recent positive characterisations of transpeople in the media (2002:134; see also Sanger 2006).
6 The Gender Recognition Act allows for transpeople to apply for a gender recognition certificate that enables them to change the gender on their birth certificates. The Civil Partnership Act enables the legal union of partners of the 'same sex'.

References

American Psychiatric Association (1994) *Diagnostic and Statistical Manual of Mental Disorders, 4th edition* (*DSM-IV*), Washington, DC: American Psychiatric Association.
Anderson, B.F. (1998) Therapeutic issues in working with transgendered clients. In D. Denny (ed.), *Current Concepts in Transgender Identity*. London: Garland, pp. 215–16.
Blanchard, R. and Collins, P.I. (1993) Men with sexual interest in transvestites, transsexuals, and she-males. *The Journal of Nervous and Mental Disease*, **181**, 570–5.
Bockting, W., Knudson, G. and Goldberg, J.M. (2006) *Counselling and Mental Health Care of Transgendered Adults and Loved Ones*. Vancouver Coastal Health. [Online] www.vch.ca/transhealth/resources/library/tcpdocs/guidelines-mental-health.pdf [accessed May 2007].
Broad, K.L. (2002) GLB+T? Gender/sexuality movements and transgender collective identity (de)constructions. *International Journal of Sexuality and Gender Studies*, **7**, 241–64.

Brown, G.R. (1998) Women in the closet: relationships with transgendered men. In D. Denny (ed.), *Current Concepts in Transgender Identity*. London: Garland, pp. 353–71.

Butler, J. (1990) *Gender Trouble: Feminism and the Subversion of Identity*. London: Routledge.

Butler, J. (2004) *Undoing Gender*. London: Routledge.

Califia, P. (1997) *Sex Changes: The Politics of Transgenderism*. San Francisco: Cleis Press.

Carroll, L., Gilroy, P.J. and Ryan, J. (2002) Counseling transgendered, transsexual and gender-variant clients. *Journal of Counseling and Development*, **80**, 131–9.

De Lauretis, T. (1991) Queer theory: lesbian and gay sexualities. *Differences: A Journal of Feminist Cultural Studies*, **3**, iii–xviii.

Denny, D. (2004) Changing models of transsexualism. *Journal of Gay and Lesbian Psychotherapy*, **8**, 25–40.

Devor, H. (1994) Sexual orientation identities, attractions and practices of female-to-male transsexuals. *The Journal of Sex Research*, **30**, 303–15.

Gagne, P., Tewksbury, R. and McGaughey, D. (1997) Coming out and crossing over: identity formation and proclamation in a transgender community. *Gender and Society*, **11**, 478–508.

Great Britain. Parliament (2004a) *Gender Recognition Act*. London: HMSO. [Online] http://www.opsi.gov.uk/acts/acts2004/20040033.htm [accessed May 2007].

Great Britain. Parliament (2004b) *Civil Partnership Act*. London: HMSO. [Online] www.opsi.gov.uk/acts/acts2004/20040007.htm [accessed May 2007].

Green, R. (1987) *The 'Sissy Boy Syndrome' and the Development of Homosexuality*. New Haven: Yale University Press.

Green, R. (1992) *Sexual Science and the Law*. Cambridge: Harvard University Press.

Hines, S. (2006) Intimate transitions: transgender practices of partnering and parenting. *Sociology*, **40**, 353–71.

Hird, M.J. (2000) Gender's nature: intersexuality, transsexualism and the 'sex/gender' binary. *Feminist Theory*, **1**, 347–64.

Hird, M.J. (2002) For a sociology of transsexualism. *Sociology*, **36**, 577–96.

Money, J. and Ehrhardt, A. (1972) *Man and Woman/Boy and Girl*. Baltimore: Johns Hopkins Press.

Namaste, V. (2000) *Invisible Lives: The Erasure of Transsexual and Transgendered People*. Chicago: University of Chicago Press.

Prosser, J. (1998) *Second Skins: The Body Narratives of Transsexuality*. New York: Columbia University Press.

Raj, R. (2002) Towards a transpositive therapeutic model – developing clinical sensitivity and cultural competence in the effective support of transsexual and transgendered clients. *The International Journal of Transgenderism*, **6**. [Online] www.symposion.com/ijt/ijtvo06no02_04.htm [accessed May 2007].

Sanger, T. (2006) *Desiring difference? Transpeople's intimate partnerships and the cultural construction of gender and sexuality*. PhD thesis, The Queen's University of Belfast.

Seidman, S. (1996) (ed.) *Queer Theory/Sociology*. Oxford, Blackwell.

Steiner, B.W. and Bernstein, S.M. (1981) Female-to-male transsexuals and their partners. *Canadian Journal of Psychology*, **26**, 178–82.

Whittle, S. (2002) *Respect and Equality: Transsexual and Transgender Rights.* London: Cavendish.

Resource list

Depend (2005) *Support for transpeople and their friends and families.* [Online] www.depend.org.uk/support.html [accessed May 2007].

Goldberg, J. (2006) *Recommended framework for training mental health clinicians in transgender care.* [Online] www.vch.ca/transhealth/resources/library/tcpdocs/training-mentalhealth.pdf [accessed May 2007].

Lev, A.I. (1998) *Guidelines for therapists working with transgender clients.* Choices Counselling and Consulting. [Online] www.choicesconsulting.com/areas/transgender/tg_therapy_guidelines.html [accessed May 2007].

Lev, A.I. (1998) *Being a good gender therapist.* Choices Counselling and Consulting. [Online] www.choicesconsulting.com/areas/transgender/good_gender_therapist.html [accessed May 2007].

Lev, A.I. (2000) *Transgendered people and their families.* Choices Counselling and Consulting. [Online] www.choicesconsulting.com/aboutarlene/articles/transgendered. html [accessed May 2007].

Mermaids (2005) *Family support group for children and teenagers with gender identity issues.* [Online] www.mermaids.freeuk.com [accessed May 2007].

Press For Change (1997) *Campaigning for respect and equality for all transpeople.* [Online] www.pfc.org.uk [accessed May 2007].

Sanctity (2005) *Group campaigning for the right of pre-existing marriages involving a transperson to continue following transition.* [Online] www.sanctity.org.uk [accessed May 2007].

Chapter 7

Queer in practice

Therapy and queer theory

Catherine Butler and Angela Byrne

As clinical psychologists in HIV and sexual health services, we have chosen to use queer theory to influence our work because it is located within a postmodern epistemology, which deconstructs and challenges normative and heteronormative discourses, including those relating to relationships and sex. A queer theory approach allows us to join with our clients in constructing new meanings and narratives outside the limiting and oppressive societal and cultural definitions of what is 'normal', 'healthy' and 'desirable'. Thus this approach provides a challenge to traditional psychological therapies which can be based on Western, heteronormative ideals. This is essential for work with our clients who often come from ethnic and sexual minority groups. In this chapter we discuss the theoretical underpinnings of our work, providing clear examples and transcript to illustrate our approach. This involves systemic and social constructionist models, as well as a queer critique of heteronormative models of sex, sexuality and relationship. We will challenge traditional notions of 'client' and 'expert' and present an alternative approach to therapeutic ethics. We will also describe some of the techniques we use to introduce a queer perspective in training psychologists.

Background

Queer theorists challenge basic assumptions about sex, gender and sexuality, including the dichotomies of heterosexual/homosexual and male/female and thus develop new ways of exploring issues of human identity and relationships (Spargo 1999) – issues that are arguably of prime importance and interest to psychologists. Yet, while queer theory has been highly influential within the fields of cultural and literary studies and philosophy, it has had less impact on the theory and practice of psychology.

'Queer' is not a term that is generally used or recognised within mainstream psychology, except perhaps to a limited extent within its academic sphere. Within training it is practically non-existent, with case studies, research subjects and issues being almost exclusively heterosexual, or the sexuality of subjects not being mentioned at all, as it is assumed they are heterosexual and that this does not need stating. Even when 'difference and diversity' modules are included in the curriculum, sexuality can exclude even more recognised categories like 'lesbian' and 'gay' (Butler 2004a), or at best given a slot for three hours on a three-year training programme. One reason for this is that the notion of 'queer' – either in its popular usage as an alternative identity or as a set of practices that unsettle assumptions about sexual identity and behaviour – cannot be easily accommodated in most psychological models. This is for a number of reasons.

First, where sexuality is addressed within psychology and psychotherapy, it is conceptualised as an individual and 'internal' attribute, i.e. individual people are described as 'heterosexual' or 'homosexual', 'gay' or 'straight'. The same is true of mainstream psychological views of gender and gender identity. In contrast, 'queer' is a socio-cultural and political concept. For example, queer theorists such as Judith Butler present gender as a 'performative effect' that is experienced by the individual as natural identity (Butler 1990). For Butler, gender is not the conceptual or cultural extension of chromosomal or biological sex but rather an ongoing discursive practice that is currently structured around the concept of heterosexuality as the norm of human relationships (Spargo 1999). The psychological view of gender and sexual identity as individual and internal has been criticised (e.g. Kitzinger 1989) as obscuring the political and allowing psychologists to ignore the mechanisms of power and oppression in the lives of their clients.

Second, as already mentioned, mainstream psychological models tend to accept the binary categories of 'male/female' and 'homosexual/heterosexual'. Traditionally, heterosexuality has been accepted as 'normal' and 'natural', while homosexuality has generally been treated as a 'problem' to be explained (nature versus nurture) or a pathology to be cured. The history of the pathologisation of lesbians, gay men and bisexuals by psychology has been extensively discussed elsewhere (e.g. Kitzinger 1990) and will not be covered in detail here. While these approaches have changed and, in the UK at least, psychologists no longer offer therapy aimed at changing someone's sexual preference, there still tends to be an acceptance of binary categories and of the idea of sexual identity as internal, individual and fixed. For example, when we turn to look at psychological approaches to transgendered identities, we can see that they are conceptualised almost totally within a medical/pathology model, i.e. the concept of 'gender dysphoria' or 'gender identity disorder' as a medical or psychiatric diagnosis (Denman 2004). In queer theory terms, psychology may thus be described as being involved in the production of knowledges that have served to reinforce the normalising of heterosexuality and gender dichotomy and the oppression of other practices and identities.

Psychology as a profession has traditionally positioned itself within a 'scientist-practitioner' model, emphasising that therapeutic practice should be based on 'scientific' psychological research. This view is associated with a positivist epistemology and the idea of the psychologist as objective observer. In line with this, the development of cognitive behavioural therapy (CBT) since the 1970s offered an alternative to psychodynamic ways of working, but one that still conceptualises problems as individual and internal, for example arising from faulty thinking patterns. CBT fits into the current climate of evidence-based practice, often viewed as the 'gold standard' within the National Health Service (NHS), our working context as clinical psychologists in the UK. Given the contexts outlined above, it is reasonable to question whether, as clinical psychologists, it is possible to be queer in practice, and if it is possible, what can that look like? In the following sections, we will outline the theoretical underpinnings of our approach to therapy and elucidate why we think this is compatible with queer theory and practices and appropriate to working with clients who have been or may be ab-normalised by mainstream psychological therapy.

An alternative approach

As therapists who have worked primarily within the NHS and also in the voluntary sector, we have met with hundreds of individuals and couples with relationship and sexual difficulties. In our work together, we have found useful alternative approaches to that provided by more traditional psychological theory. We base our work on social constructionist principles, as developed and operationalised with post-Milan systemic therapy and narrative therapy. Systemic therapy was developed in theory and practice by a team of four psychotherapists – Cecchin, Bocoloio, Prata and Selvini-Palazzoli – based in Milan during the 1970s and 80s. Their ideas were mainly inspired by the work of communication theorist Gregory Bateson, who emphasised the importance of attending to 'the difference that makes the difference' (Bateson 1972) in that change occurs when people experience its possibility. In the 1980s, the rise of postmodernist thinking, particularly social constructionism and feminist theory, shaped systemic therapy further as it entered the 'post-Milan' era. Systemic therapy of the 1990s and beyond takes account of power and social differences in ways that we feel complement queer theory and our work with lesbian, gay, bisexual and trans clients. It allows for a different perspective on therapist–client relationships and practices, with particular emphasis on power relations, knowledge and language (Simon and Whitfield 2000). This model also acknowledges and accommodates the importance of self-reflectivity, which we feel is essential for practitioners both in clinical work and research. Our own self-reflections on how we are positioned in our work and the key connections between these two approaches are now discussed.

A postmodern approach

Postmodernism has provided a critique of the notions of universal truths, scientific method and objectivity (Simon and Whitfield 2000). Within this critique, an individual's 'realities' are socially constructed and constituted through language and discourse and there are no essential truths. This approach stands in contrast to a positivist epistemology and instead invites a reflexive way of knowing that recognises how therapists are inevitably acting out of their own beliefs, cultural context and experience. These will influence the conversation we have with clients and the meaning we jointly construct around the topic discussed. Wittgenstein (1952) refers to this as the creation of local knowledges, to recognise that meaning arises through language use within local contexts and not by finite, universal definitions of words. Therefore, we do not consider ourselves to be objective observers but part of the 'system' that is operating in the client's life.

Queer theory itself is under the umbrella of postmodernism, where universal truths or structures give way to a 'multiverse' or plurality of ideas about the world (Lax 1992), and so different realities are recognised as being equally valid. For example, it is considered that there are multiple ways to 'perform gender' or to conduct relationships. This approach is critical to our work as it allows us to take a non-heteronormative stance. And so we may work with people who choose a variety of relationship structures, e.g. non-monogamy, or those who do not engage in penetrative sex (vaginally or anally). We would see our task in therapy as clarifying the sexual and relational choices that each member makes so that the relationship of choice is negotiated and understood by all involved. The following example shows why and how two men brought their issues to Angela.

Jonathan, a 35-year-old white British man, and Kai, a 40-year-old Thai man, attended for therapy due to increasing conflict in their relationship. They reported that for the first two years of their relationship they were very happy and experienced little conflict. During this time they described themselves as 'fuck buddies'. Several months ago, they decided to become 'boyfriends'. It was soon after this that they began to have arguments. Kai reported that Jonathan was constantly calling and texting him throughout the day, and he felt that he was being checked up on. Jonathan reported that he felt extremely anxious when they were apart. He was worried that Kai was going to saunas to have sex and felt Kai withdrawing from him, resulting in feelings of panic. Below is an example of a conversation aimed at exploring and clarifying their relational choices.

AB: How was it decided that you would become 'boyfriends'?

Jonathan: Well, I guess it was my idea but I think we both agreed on it.

             (Kai nods)

AB: How did you see things changing when you became 'boyfriends'?

Jonathan: Well, I think it means that you do things together and that it's not just about sex anymore.

AB: How about you, Kai? What does being 'boyfriends' mean to you?

Kai: It does mean doing things together but still having your own life. I think sex is still really important and now it feels like certain things are off limits. . . .

Jonathan: What do you mean?

Kai: Like, we used to go to the sauna together, but that doesn't happen any more.

Jonathan: But that's not really what boyfriends do, is it?

AB: It sounds like you might have some different ideas about what being boyfriends means. I was wondering where do your ideas come from about what it means to be boyfriends?

Jonathan: I don't know really. I suppose I think about my sister and her husband. They're very close and do everything together . . . and my parents are still together and . . . I suppose it's just something you aspire to.

Kai: But they're straight. It's not really the same is it? Most of the long-term gay couples I know don't have sex with each other anymore, and that's not what we want. I had that with my partner, Richard, but I think 'boyfriends' is different. It means we still have sex.

Jonathan: I kind of think of 'partners' and 'boyfriends' as the same.

AB: How was it when you were 'fuck buddies'?

Jonathan: We knew where we stood then.

Kai: Yes. The rules were pretty clear so we never had problems.

AB: What do you think helped you to be clear?

Kai: Well, we've both been on the scene for a while. Everybody knows what 'fuck buddies' means. It's like you agree to meet when its mutually convenient and you don't have any other expectations of it.

Jonathan: But also we talked about it and agreed. I guess we never really talked about what being boyfriends would mean before.

AB: If we were to imagine a definition of 'boyfriends' that
           would be relevant to you as gay men, what might that look
           like?

A 'non-expert' stance

Traditionally, psychologists have taken an 'expert' position in therapy, e.g.
helping clients to adjust their 'negative automatic thoughts' or interpreting
'transference' in the therapy room. In contrast, systemic and social constructionist therapists take a 'non-expert' or 'not-knowing' stance (Anderson
and Goolishian 1992). In other words, while we have knowledge of, or
'expertise' in, the process of therapy, the client is the expert on their own
meaning and experience, not the therapist. By positioning ourselves as non-
expert, we thus acknowledge and respect the choices and power of the client.
Our mindfulness in how this stance positions ourselves and the client fits
with Foucault's (1978) ideas that power is relational and not the possession
of an individual. We therefore cannot 'empower' clients, which would imply
we have power to give them, but position ourselves in a way that draws on
the power they use to make life choices. Foucault suggested that we can
never be free of power but can resist it when it is oppressive. Queer theorists
(e.g. Sedgwick 1990; Halperin 1995) applied these ideas to heterosexism,
while feminist theorists (e.g. Haraway 1991) have used them to challenge
patriarchy (Minton 1997). An example of how this resistance can be used
therapeutically, is to ask 'what is the problem and for whom?'. This
acknowledges that it is the dominant majority who often define a problem,
e.g. non-monogamy being described as 'promiscuity' when compared to
heteronormative ideas of marriage and commitment.

   What is queer is therefore that which is subjugated in relation to that
which is dominant, not the affirmation of an alternative identity: it is to be
'other'. This idea becomes very interesting when applied to the context in
which we work, HIV/sexual health services, as staff and clients often hold
multiple and overlapping roles: as service users, service providers, volunteers and campaigners. In addition, contributing to and because of the
culture of sexual health services, many lesbians, gay men and bisexuals
choose to work in this area. This can result in an overlap between a therapist's personal and professional life (for a detailed examination of this
issue, see Taylor, Slots, Roberts and Maddicks, 1998, who describe their
work as gay therapists who see gay clients and share the 'scene' in Brighton).
Similarly, the advent of the Gaydar web site and similar sites creates additional possibilities for clients and therapists to be exposed to each others'
sexuality, which will need to be addressed in the context of therapeutic
boundaries and ethics. The recognition and acceptance of these dual roles

contributes to the therapist not 'othering' the client through subjugation by taking an expert role.

Clients may also live their relationships in ways that do not mirror our own relationship choices, and we would try to celebrate rather than pathologise this difference. Our curiosity and respect about the choices clients make move us away from 'norm-based' ideas of sex and relationships. We can ask questions that validate and support client decisions, as well as assisting clarity and revision, such as 'As a couple, how did you negotiate the rules of your non-monogamy?'. By recognising the fluidity of people's lives, identities and practices, we can help them affirm the choices they have made for their life at this time, and not impose cultural or heteronormative ideas of how relationships should develop. The following example involves a heterosexual couple who worked for over a year with Catherine.

Fatima and Abdul were referred for therapy with CB because they had not had penetrative sex for three years. Fatima had been raped by a gang of soldiers in their country of origin, and the couple had come to England to seek asylum. They were both strict Muslims and when asked why penetrative sex was important, Fatima explained that it was her duty as a wife and they hoped to have children in the future. Sex was therefore not seen as something that was for pleasure, which conflicted with CB's feminist views. The couple also told CB that the idea of 'foreplay' would not be acceptable to them, because it was for pleasure, which made following a step-wise typical sex therapy programme difficult. CB took a transparent perspective and spoke about the differences in their views given their cultural and religious differences. This allowed CB to investigate other ideas within the Muslim faith around sex, and she discovered two important pieces of information – that foreplay is permitted within a marriage if performed as a couple and not as masturbation, and that if there is a medical reason, decrees from the Koran can be set aside (e.g. a diabetic can eat in Ramadan). By taking a non-expert stance and presenting this information as ideas that CB had come across, an opportunity was created for the couple to discuss exercises in touching that would be acceptable to them, if not placed under the title of foreplay. The couple began a programme of mutual massage and Fatima began to explore her genitals. CB also explained to the couple that Fatima could still get pregnant without penetrative sex if they used a syringe to insert the sperm. The couple rejected this idea at first. However, as Fatima became able to insert her finger into her vagina, they spoke again about using syringes to get pregnant, not telling CB they had this discussion. CB was therefore extremely surprised when Fatima started a session by announcing that she was six weeks pregnant, while they still had not had penetrative sex! One of the meanings behind why penetrative sex was important had therefore been achieved, and Fatima was also fulfilling her duty as a wife by providing Abdul with a child. The couple therefore used CB's ideas as suggestions to draw out their own resourcefulness and ability to communicate and create solutions to find a way to be intimate and have children, without penetrative sex.

Multiple perspectives

In line with queer resistance of the dominant norm, Maturana (1978) has influenced systemic therapy with his ideas of multiple perspectives. He suggests that reality is a 'multiverse', rather than a 'universe', as there is not one true reality but multiple possibilities. Thus, we acknowledge that as therapists our ideas about the world and lived experience may be different in more or less ways to the ideas and lived experiences of our clients. This perspective provides a means of resisting subjugated discourses that clients may present with. This is illustrated below with the example of a client who met with Catherine saying she was 'confused' about her sexuality.

Athena presented for therapy with CB because she was 'confused about her sexuality'. She had been a strict Christian all her life and had recently had penetrative vaginal sex with a man for the first time (she was in her 40s). However, the man she had started a sexual relationship with was married, which troubled her. Her confusion was around the fact that she was enjoying a new-found sense of her sexuality but felt guilty about the circumstances as it conflicted with her morality as learnt within her church. She had spoken to her church leader about this and was advised to stop attending her church until the relationship had ended. The multiple perspectives on her current situation were in conflict. In therapy, I was also influenced in hearing her story (as you are in reading it) by my own multiple perspectives, which for me included being agnostic and sexually active. By acknowledging there were different views about her situation, both within the room and within different parts of her community, we could examine which ideas she found more or less helpful and so which she might hold onto or reject. An example of this conversation follows.

Athena: I don't want to give this up, he makes me feel alive in a way I have never felt before. But, at the same time, he is married, so I am breaking one of the Ten Commandments.

CB: Who else might share this view?

Athena: Well the church. This is what is so painful. To be with him I have to forfeit the community that has given me support and love all of my life. But the thought of being without him is also so painful.

CB: And is there anyone who might have a different view to this?

Athena: Well, I told my brother. He is not religious and he was happy for me. But I don't think he understands.

CB: You know I am not religious. Do you feel that I can understand the dilemma you find yourself in?

Athena: I think it helps that you are not in the church because I do not feel that you are judging me. You might think I'm being silly though because I am obviously older than you?

CB: I don't think you are silly but it seems as if you are struggling to bring together these two parts of your identity that are important to you: your relationship with God and your relationship with this man. Do you still feel you have a relationship with God, even if your relationship with the church has been damaged?

Athena: I hadn't thought of that before. Yes, I still pray everyday and ask his forgiveness and guidance on what I should do.

CB: I'm not sure how these things work (laughter) but have you had some answers or suggestions?

Athena: (laughter) Well I guess I still feel close to God, despite this. I still feel his love, and he is a forgiving God.

CB: So is it possible to keep your relationship with God, while you explore this sexual part of yourself?

Athena: It is not ideal, but my situation feels different to what I had expected from my life anyway. I always thought I would be married with children at this age.

CB: So maybe there are ways of doing things differently to what is expected. What other examples of this can you think of?

Levels of context

Different perspectives are also considered if we examine how different contexts influence meaning-making. Cronen and Pearce (1980, 1985) developed a framework for considering which contexts influence meaning-making and how these contexts relate to each other. Their model, the coordinated management of meaning (CMM), considers that contexts determine social meanings and actions developed from Bateson's (1972) statement that 'without context there is no meaning'. This model was originally developed in a hierarchical format (Cronen and Pearce 1985):

The hierarchical model of coordinated management of meaning

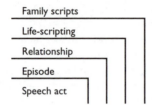

Speech acts occur within episodes of interaction that are defined and organised by the relationship between speakers that is shaped by stories of possibility from the family of origin. In later uses of the model, the contextual layer of 'culture' was added to specify that all the above occurs in a specific cultural context (e.g. Pearce 1994). These layers of meaning will be influencing each member of a conversation as it progresses. We therefore consider both the contextual influences on our meaning-making, as well as asking questions to consider how these will be influencing the meaning-making of the client. For example:

> "How is your interest in sadomasochistic practices received within your relationships?
> Within the ideas of your family of origin?
> Within lesbian culture?
> Within British culture?"
> "Which of these messages do you find most supportive / helpful?"
> "What alternatives to the judgemental messages might be possible within that same culture / family / relationship?"

This thus fits with queer ideas of resisting 'norm-based' dominant cultural messages. This approach is demonstrated below in individual therapy with Angela.

Jose, a 32-year-old Spanish gay man, was referred for therapy for depression by his HIV physician. In the referral, the doctor noted that Jose 'takes part in self-destructive sexual practices' and speculated that this was the source of his Hepatitis C infection. Jose mentioned that he was referred for therapy previously by his GP but that he didn't find it helpful. He said the therapist didn't really understand him. After a number of sessions, he began to discuss his sexual relationship and said that he felt he had a 'problem with sex'. The therapist (AB) asked when he started thinking that he had a 'problem with sex'. Jose said that he had enjoyed SM sex for a number of years and met his current partner, Peter, at an SM club. They regularly brought other men home to 'play', and Jose often felt inadequate in these scenarios. He felt criticised by Peter for not being adventurous enough and often felt low afterwards. When he discussed this with his previous therapist, she speculated that his interest in SM practices was a form of 'internalised homophobia', or an expression of guilt for his homosexuality and something that prevented him and Peter having a healthy, intimate relationship. AB wondered aloud who the SM was a problem for and who was most and least concerned about it? Through this process of deconstructive questioning, Jose identified that the 'problem' for him was not the SM practices (which he had always enjoyed) but the extent to which he felt criticised by Peter. It emerged that this criticism was apparent in other situations too and the focus of the work became how Jose could assert his needs and resist criticism, both in his sexual relationships and in other areas of his life.

The use of teams

Another example of the valuing of multiple perspectives is the use of teams in narrative and systemic therapies, generally referred to as 'reflecting teams' (e.g. Andersen 1987). Teams have commonly been used throughout the history of family therapy, where a team of therapists traditionally observe the therapist and clients from behind a one-way mirror, invisible to the clients, and deliver messages or interventions to the therapist from their 'expert' position. In contrast, teams are used by post-Milan systemic and narrative models of therapy with the aim of increasing transparency and bringing multiple perspectives to the client's circumstance. In these approaches, the team is often in the room with the client and therapist, who are invited to listen to the team's reflections after which the client is invited to comment on what they heard. The client listens to these views from their position as expert on themselves, and so they are invited to reject, expand or just comment on the observations of team members. Team members may locate the position they speak from, for example, 'as a single gay man, I was struck by Tony's thoughtfulness in his preparations for sexual encounters' or 'as a bisexual woman, I was left wondering how Annie's expectations of her partner might be different if her partner was male'.

Some narrative therapists have expanded this idea to involve teams whose members may share the issue of concern with the client e.g. women who have recovered from anorexia (Madigan and Epston 1995). This practice has been termed using 'outsider witnessing' groups. The purpose of such groups is to recruit an appropriate and supportive audience for the development of the clients' preferred futures. Such practices fit within the queer agenda of resisting, undermining and providing alternative views to dominant, heteronormative practices in therapy.

Deconstructionist practices

Like queer theories, social constructionist and systemic therapists are influenced by the work of Foucault in his examination of the various ways that people in Western societies have been categorised as 'normal' and 'abnormal'. His work examines madness (Foucault 1965), illness, (1973), criminality (1977) and sexuality (1978) as concepts around which people have been labelled as insane, sick, criminal or perverted and describes the various oppressive practices that have proceeded from that labelling. Within a Foucauldian analysis, 'language is an instrument of power and people have power in society in direct proportion to their ability to participate in the various discourses that shape that society' (Freedman and Combs 1996:37–8). Following the work of Foucault, Michael White (e.g. White 1992) has discussed the idea that we tend to internalise the dominant narratives of our culture. Social constructionist and systemic therapies aim to deconstruct these narratives in ways that are in line with queer theory, in that we put the dominant narratives under the microscope for inspection and not those of 'the other'. For example, we would not ask 'Why are some people gay?' but 'How does heterosexuality become such a prized commodity?'. We therefore use deconstructive questioning to challenge and resist oppressive dominant discourses. Catherine illustrates this in her work with a single man below.

Sam, a 35-year-old black British gay man, requested therapy because he felt unable to have sexual encounters since being diagnosed with HIV one and a half years ago. Sam no longer felt able to flirt and if someone 'hit on' him in a club he would leave feeling annoyed with himself. He felt as if 'someone poured a bucket of cold water on me' and the smallest hint at sex reminded him that he was HIV positive. This had two effects: first he assumed he would be rejected because of his HIV status, and second he 'no longer felt good enough anymore'.

We started by deconstructing the idea that he was no longer good enough. Through questioning Sam about the qualities that he brings to his friendships and relationships, Sam agreed that he would make a good boyfriend because he was loyal, honest, clear and interesting. He also discovered that he must have self-respect because he was turning down people who approached him in clubs because they just wanted 'his body', and he felt he had more to offer. What was interesting was that his friends refused to believe that he was not having sexual encounters with people but had for some reason stopped telling them about it. This alternative view of him held by his friends allowed us to deconstruct the idea that he would be rejected because of his HIV status. Midway through therapy, Sam reported that he had managed to stay in a club until closing and had flirted with others. CB questioned him about what it was about him as a person that would help her understand how he was managing to make these changes. Sam explained that he had had previous experience of adjusting to holding a minority status (how he was now seeing his HIV status). Sam spoke about his experiences of coming out to his family and of being black on the gay scene in London in the 1980s. He had recently bumped into someone he knew from a black gay support group he had attended in the 80s and was surprised to hear that he had been this man's role model because of his courage in telling his family.

Deconstructive questions and drawing on the views of other people in Sam's life allowed Sam to rediscover a story of himself as someone who had choices and courage and was experienced in disclosure and holding minority identities that he could feel ok about, even if met with disapproval from others. At the end of therapy he had started a new relationship, which he said felt like a 'training wheel'. Most importantly, Sam said he was 'not prepared to put myself in the bargain bin anymore'.

Political and ethical stance

Social constructionist and systemic approaches to therapy do not claim to be politically neutral but actively concern themselves with ethics and the politics of power. Following Foucault, theorists like Michael White have proposed that therapy can bring about 'an insurrection of subjugated knowledges' (Foucault 1980:80–4) that allows people to lay claim to the many possibilities in their lives that lie beyond the dominant narratives.

Freedman and Combs (1996) discuss the ethics of postmodernism and therapeutic approaches. They contrast these with modernist ethics, which tend to be based in rules that can be prescribed and reinforced in a 'top down' manner. While we are all bound by our professional ethics and codes of conduct, systemic therapists are also interested in a different idea of ethics, which takes account of power, social difference and context. Some critics have expressed concern that postmodern approaches are morally relativist and imply that one story or explanation is as good as another. However, as Freedman and Combs (1996) explain, ethics in this sense involve examining our beliefs and values, rather than taking them for granted and taking an explicit stance of making room for marginalised voices and cultures. These ideas have been essential for us as we both chose to work in sexual health services because of the diversity within the client group and the political and international nature of HIV.

Queer(y)ing psychology training

One of our important roles is in contributing to the training of post-graduate psychologists. In 2006 the HIV and Sexual Health Faculty of the BPS conducted a survey of all 33 clinical psychology training courses in Britain (details of the survey can be found on the faculty web site: www.bps.org.uk/dcp-sexhealth/publications/publications_home.cfm). Of the 75 per cent of courses contacted that responded, 86 per cent taught trainees how to talk to their clients about sex in therapy. While 78 per cent of the courses that responded integrated sexual diversity into their teaching, only 56 per cent of courses explicitly covered working with lesbian and gay clients. Similarly, only 47 per cent discussed sexuality within a cultural context.

In the sessions we are invited to run, we try to introduce a social constructionist and queer perspective in a number of ways:

- We locate our perspectives by disclosing our own sexualities and the possibility of their fluidity and influences on this topic (e.g. work context, politics, ethnicity, age). Also stating that we are not taking an 'expert' position and inviting participants to contribute their views throughout.
- We present historical and cultural understandings of sexuality from a Foucauldian perspective.
- We present a continuum model of sexuality that emphasises fluidity and change (e.g. Klein, Sepekoff and Wolf 1990).
- We examine discourses supporting oppressive practices towards lesbians, gay men and bisexuals by looking at stereotypes and considering representations in popular media, for example the portrayal of lesbians, gay men or bisexuals as tragic, tormented or predatory figures in popular films.
- We abnormalise the 'normal' and expose the social and cultural practices that sustain a view of heterosexuality as 'natural' or 'normal' but present 'a-day-in-the-life-of' a heterosexual person in a world where the norm is to be homosexual (Butler 2004b).

- We put heterosexuality under the microscope by asking participants to consider how heterosexual privilege influences their lives e.g. by use of the 'heterosexual questionnaire' (Rochlin 1992), which asks heterosexuals questions that are usually asked of queer people (such as 'when did you first know you were straight) and heterosexual privilege (Bohan 1996), which lists unreflected upon privileges experienced by heterosexuals (such as having role models from childhood who show your affectional and sexual orientation is normal).
- We present case vignettes that consider how the 'norms' and social messages about sexuality might be conceived of differently and so impact on clients lives in various way, through the lens of old age, adolescence, ethnic minority, learning disability, and thus introduce the notion of levels of context and multiple identities.

Our aim is to encourage a questioning and deconstructive stance in workshop participants in order to ask clients about their individual contextual influences on their sexuality, rather than accepting heteronormative ideas from which to judge others who do not fit within this box.

Conclusion

Queer theory provides an informative and creative complement to social constructionist and systemic ways of working with clients and in the training of therapists. It lends richness to deconstruction by emphasising heteronormative power and the oppressive practices that influence our clients' lives. We find such an approach essential in our work with clients, most of whom do not fit within dominant social groups, e.g. white and heterosexual. It is perhaps because of these differences that clients feel troubled and present for therapy. However, by validating the client's sexual and relationship choices by deconstructing norm-based messages and positioning the client as an expert on themselves, our clients find ways to resist oppressive narratives and continue to develop and practise their sexual and relational lives as they desire.

References

Andersen, T. (1987) The reflecting team: dialogue and meta-dialogue in clinical work. *Family Process*, **26**, 415–28.

Anderson, H. and Goolishian, H. (1992) The client is the expert: a not-knowing approach to therapy. In S. McNamee and K. Gergen (eds), *Therapy as Social Construction*. London: Sage, pp. 24–39.

Bateson, G. (1972) *Steps to an Ecology of Mind*. New York: Ballentine.

Bohan, J.S. (1996) *Psychology and Sexual Orientation: Coming to Terms*. New York: Routledge.

Butler, C. (2004a) Lesbian and gay trainees: the challenges of personal and professional integration. *Lesbian and Gay Psychology Review*, **5**(1), 22–9.

Butler, C. (2004b) An awareness-raising tool addressing lesbian and gay lives. *Clinical Psychology*, **36**, 15–17.

Butler, J. (1990) *Gender Trouble: Feminism and the Subversion of Identity*. London: Routledge.

Cronen, V. and Pearce, W.B. (1980) *Communication, Action and Meaning: The Creation of Social Realities*. New York: Praeger.

Cronen, V.E. and Pearce, W.B. (1985) Toward an explanation of how the Milan method words: an invitation to a systemic epistemology and the evolution of family systems. In D. Campbell and R. Drapers (eds), *Applications of Systemic Family Therapy: The Milan Approach*. London: Grune and Gratton.

Denman, C. (2004) *Sexuality: A Biopsychosocial Approach*. Hampshire: Macmillan.

Foucault, M. (1965) *Madness and Civilisation*. New York: Pantheon.

Foucault, M. (1973) *Birth of the Clinic*. New York: Pantheon.

Foucault, M. (1977) *Discipline and Punish*. New York: Pantheon.

Foucault, M. (1978) *The History of Sexuality: An Introduction*, vol. 1. New York: Random House.

Foucault, M. (1980) *Power/Knowledge: Selected Interviews and Other Writings*. New York: Pantheon.

Freedman, J. and Combs, G. (1996) *The Social Construction of Preferred Realities*. New York: W.W. Norton.

Halperin, D.M. (1995) *Saint Foucault: Towards a Gay Hagiography*. Oxford: Oxford University Press.

Haraway, D.J. (1991) A cyborg manifesto. In D.J. Haraway (ed.), *Simians, Cyborgs and Women*. New York: Routledge, pp. 149–81.

Kitzinger, C. (1989) Liberal humanism as an ideology of control: the regulation of lesbian identities. In J. Shotter and K. Gergen (eds), *Texts of Identity*. London: Sage, pp. 82–98.

Kitzinger, C. (1990) Heterosexism in psychology. *The Psychologist*, **3**, 391–2.

Klein, F., Sepekoff, B. and Wolf, T.J. (1990) Sexual orientation: a multi-variable dynamic process. In T. Geller (ed.), *Bisexuality: A Reader and Sourcebook*. Albion, CA: Times Change Press, pp. 35–49.

Lax, W.D. (1992) Postmodern thinking in clinical practice. In S. McNamee and K. Gergen (eds), *Therapy as Social Construction*. London: Sage.

Madigan, S. and Epston, D. (1995) From Spychiartric gaze to communities of concern: from professional monologue to dialogue. In S. Friedman (ed.), *The Reflecting Team in Action*. New York: Guilford Press, pp. 257–76.

Maturana, H.R. (1978) Biology of language: the epistemology of reality. In G.A. Miller and E. Lennenberg (eds), *Psychology and Biology of Language and Thought*. New York: Academic Press, pp. 27–63.

Minton, H.L. (1997) Queer theory: historical roots and implications for psychology. *Theory and Psychology*, **7**, 337–53.

Pearce, W.B. (1994) *Interpersonal Communication: Making Social Worlds*. New York: Harper Collins.

Rochlin, M. (1992) Heterosexual questionnaire. In W. Blumenfeld (ed.), *Homphobia: How We All Pay the Price*. Boston: Beacon Press, pp. 203–4.

Sedgwick, E.K. (1990) *The Epistemology of the Closet.* Berkeley: University of California Press.

Simon, G. and Whitfield, G. (2000) Social constructionist and systemic therapy. In D. Davies and C. Neal (eds), *Pink Therapy 2: Therapeutic Perspectives on Working with Lesbian, Gay and Bisexual Clients.* Buckingham: Open University Press, pp. 144–62.

Spargo, T. (1999) *Postmodern Encounters: Foucault and Queer Theory.* Cambridge: Icon Books.

Taylor, G., Slots, B., Roberts, B. and Maddicks, R. (1998) A queer business: gay clinicians working with gay clients. *Clinical Psychology Forum,* **119**, 9–13.

White, M. (1992) Deconstruction and therapy. In D. Epston and M. White (eds), *Experience, Contradiction, Narrative and Imagination: Selected Papers of David Epston and Michael White 1989–1991.* Adelaide: Dulwich Centre Publication, pp. 109–51.

Wittgenstein, L. (1952) *Philosophical Investigations.* Oxford: Blackwell.

Chapter 8

Kinky clients, kinky counselling?

The challenges and potentials of BDSM

Meg Barker, Alessandra Iantaffi and Camel Gupta

> Most people find it difficult to grasp that whatever they like to do sexually will be thoroughly repulsive to someone else, and that whatever repels them sexually will be the most treasured delight of someone, somewhere . . . Most people mistake their sexual preferences for a universal system that will or should work for everyone.
>
> Rubin (1984:283)

One of the most demonised forms of consensual sexuality is bondage and discipline, domination and submission, and sadomasochism (BDSM). Many counsellors still consider it appropriate to make negative comments about BDSM in a way that is perceived to be unacceptable in relation to other aspects of sexuality (Hudson-Allez 2005). Kolmes, Stock and Moser (2006:315) found 118 reports of 'biased or inadequate' care from psycho-therapists in their survey of 175 BDSM clients. These may be rooted in the threat posed by 'queer' sexualities that trouble the binary constructions of gender and sexuality underlying conventional heterosexuality (Barker 2003). It may also relate to perceptions of BDSM as inherently sexual, which make claims for citizenship amongst BDSM practitioners proble-matic (Langdridge and Butt 2004, 2005).

In this chapter we briefly present the current legal and clinical status of BDSM, revisiting and updating some of the material included in Bridoux's (2000) chapter on this issue. We consider why BDSM might be perceived as particularly threatening, exploring the extent to which in can be seen as a queer sexuality that challenges heteronormativity. Focusing on an example text, we consider how BDSM is currently presented to counsellors and psychotherapists. We also report on the literature covering negative clients' experiences, which illustrates the perpetuation of prevalent demonising and pathologising discourses in therapy (Kolmes, Stock and Moser 2006). Drawing on the existing, but limited, non-pathologising literature on psychotherapeutic issues with BDSM clients, and social constructionist approaches to psychotherapy, we then suggest good practice for therapists working with clients who practise BDSM.

Introducing BDSM

BDSM is a term used to encompass various activities. These generally involve the exchange of some form of power or pain, often, but not exclusively, in a sexual context. Authors on the topic sometimes use the abbreviation SM or S/M to refer to the same range of practices (Langdridge and Barker 2005; Kleinplatz and Moser 2006), but BDSM seems to be a more encompassing term preferred amongst the communities involved (Informed Consent 2006). It can be difficult for those unfamiliar with such practices to conceptualise what is meant by 'power' and 'pain' in this context and to understand how they might be experienced positively by anyone. However, some degree of power or pain exchange is common in many people's sexual practices. For example, biting or light spanking, role-playing school-girls or doctors, or holding a partner down by the wrists during sex because both parties find this desirable and exciting. BDSM codifies such practices more explicitly and uses terminology such as 'power' or 'pain' exchange in negotiation between partners and in community-based literature so that there is a shared understanding (see Appendix for examples of BDSM scenarios).

Some regard BDSM as an integral part of their sexual identity while others view it more as an activity they practice.[1] This mirrors most sexual identities and means that, while it is possible to make some general comments, it is important for therapists to remain aware that, much as one would not assume that the heterosexuality of a monogamous couple in their 70s who had been married for 50 years would necessarily have large areas of commonality with that of a polyamorous triad in their 20s, BDSM is an umbrella term for a type of dynamic and/or identity that is subject to modification by the other groupings within which clients find themselves.

Janus and Janus (1994) report that up to 14 per cent of American men and 11 per cent of American women have engaged in some form of BDSM sexual behaviour and estimates of the extent of BDSM fantasy are much higher. Kleinplatz and Moser (2006) point to the fact that BDSM organisations and events exist throughout the US, UK and in many other Western countries, and there is a huge variety of BDSM-related materials available in adult stores and on the 27 million or so web pages devoted to the topic.

Langdridge and Butt (2004) suggest that stories of BDSM are having 'their time' to be heard at the start of the twenty-first century (Plummer 1995), with BDSM themes now commonplace in popular TV programmes and widely released American movies (e.g. *Will and Grace*, 2001; *Buffy the Vampire Slayer*, 2001; *Secretary*, 2002; *Kill Bill*, 2003). BDSM has been commodified to sell everything from yoghurt to supermarkets (Beckmann 2001; Sisson 2005). It could be argued that it is not BDSM practices per se but rather the imagery associated with BDSM (e.g. accessories like handcuffs and riding crops) and the way it is signified on the body (e.g. materials like leather and PVC and body piercing), which have become more visible and therefore more acceptable in a mainstream context. High Street sex shops and popular magazines now encourage heterosexual women to incorporate 'kinky' practices to spice up their monogamous sex lives and keep their partners interested (e.g. *Scarlet* magazine 2005) while policing the boundaries against 'real' BDSM (Storr 2003). Weiss (2006) reports that mainstream media representations of BDSM are still on the increase, although they, and their viewers, tend to either normalise or pathologise it. Normalisation can be seen in the otherwise traditional heterosexual love story of *Secretary* (2002) and pathologisation in crime dramas such as *Wire in the Blood* (2002), which links BDSM to mental illness, sexual abuse and murder. Weiss reports that such pathologising representations tend to occur when BDSM falls, in other respects, outside of Rubin's (1984) charmed circle of sexual relationships, that is, for example, by being non-heterosexual or non-monogamous.

BDSM practices are still restricted legally in countries worldwide, and prosecutions are on the increase in the US (Ridinger 2006). In the UK Spanner case (Regina v. Brown 1990),[2] 16 men were charged. The judge, Mr. James Rant, QC, declared that consent was not an eligible defence and the defendants had to plead guilty and serve prison sentences either for assault or, in the case of the 'bottoms',[3] for 'aiding and abetting an assault'. The European Court of Human Rights upheld this decision in 1997 (Chaline, 2005). However, in Canada in 2004 a judge ruled that BDSM videos seized by police were not obscene and that BDSM is a 'normal and acceptable' part of human sexuality based on consensual play and not violence (*Toronto News* 2004). Rubin (1984) points out that BDSM generally results in far less severe injuries than sports such as boxing and football, and BDSMers do not frequent emergency departments more than anyone else (Moser 2002). However, boxers are seen as 'sane' and consenting under the law whereas BDSMers are not.

BDSM is also still pathologised in the *American Psychiatric Association Diagnostic and Statistical Manual* (*DSM-IV-TR*),[4] with sexual sadism and masochism being listed as 'paraphilias' (302.83, 302.84). These are defined as people having 'sexual fantasies, urges or behaviours which involve inflicting (or having inflicted on oneself) psychological or physical suffering to enhance or achieve sexual excitement' (including being beaten, humiliated, bound or tortured). This has to have lasted for at least six months and to have caused 'marked distress or interpersonal difficulty'. These definitions are problematic because they equate BDSM with non-consensual 'disorders' (paedophilia, voyeurism) and suggest that BDSMers are more psychologically unhealthy than others, when there is no empirical evidence to support this (Gosselin and Wilson 1980; Moser and Levitt 1987). Also, because of the taboos around BDSM in our culture, being involved in BDSM may well involve 'significant distress or impairment in . . . functioning' for a time, precisely because of the stigma, social unacceptability, discrimination and prejudice surrounding it. Kleinplatz and Moser (2005) present further compelling arguments for the complete depathologisation of BDSM, likening its inclusion in the *DSM* to that of homosexuality until 1973 (Kutchins and Kirk 1997) and questioning the implication that BDSMers require explaining, treating and curing.

There is also a linguistic slippage which is rarely questioned between sexual sadism as an act whose erotic charge is gained precisely from its *nonconsensual* status, and sadism and masochism in BDSM where the explicitly negotiated or agreed status of the act is key to the sexual excitement potentially experienced by the practitioner. There is an illogical conflation of a crime of violence exerted via sexual means and a 'safe, sane and consensual' practice undertaken by two or more consenting adults (Keinplatz and Moser 2006). A comparable situation would be to equate a subject for whom sexual excitement was a primary motivation to rape and consenting sexual activity between adults. There is little evidence to connect the two behaviours (Baggaley 2006; Kleinplatz and Moser 2006). The psychiatrist Chess Denman (2004) makes a persuasive case for the separation of 'transgressive' and 'coercive' practices.

BDSM as queer[5]

Some authors have explained the continued negative perceptions of BDSM, and its continued criminalisation and pathologisation, in terms of the threat posed by 'queer' sexualities which challenge heteronormativity (Sullivan 2003).

Freud (1905) saw sadism and masochism as 'sexual aberrations' because they deviated from the 'normal' sexual aim (penile-vaginal penetration). Such theories have shaped dominant understandings of sexuality and Califia (1980:141) argues that 'vanilla[6] heterosexuality is still the psychiatric gold standard' and that mental health professionals generally do not question this received wisdom. Reiersøl and Skeid (2006) agree that current nosologies of sexual disorders are based on notion that heterosexual intercourse is the ideal. BDSM can be seen as queer in the popular sense that it performs a function in this discourse as one of the transgressive behaviours against which the dominant norm can define (Califia 1980).

As well as challenging Freud's 'normal sexual aim', writers have argued that BDSM also threatens his 'normal sexual object' (the 'opposite sex') since it can enable people to play with gendered notions of dominance and submission and activity and passivity (in combinations involving a man and a woman as well as in same-sex, transgendered and multiple partner combinations). Taylor and Ussher's (2001) female participants spoke of BDSM sex meaning that they could dominate men and be the ones with the 'cock'.

It seems clear how BDSM situations involving women 'topping' can challenge traditional gender roles in sex, however, participants also speak of man-dominant-woman-submissive BDSM as 'parodying sexual relations considered as traditionally subjugating, oppressive and exploitative of women' (p. 303) and presented it in a rather 'queer' way as ridiculing, undermining, exposing and destroying the traditional man–woman power dynamics inherent in heteronormativity (Ritchie and Barker 2005). Further, BDSM potentially (although not inevitably) provides an alternative to strong narratives of sex as genitally focused, as well as severely disrupting narratives of reproduction in otherwise notionally heterosexual sex encounters (Califia 1980).

Linked to this, theorists have argued that the common description of BDSM as 'play' and the assignment of roles involved also render it queer. Foucault stated: '[T]he S&M game is very interesting because . . . it is always fluid. Of course, there are roles, but everybody knows very well that those roles can be reversed' (Macey 1993:368–9). BDSM could be seen as part of a queer critique of humanist, individualist notions of one, coherent self. It could be seen as a subversive form of 'self-fashioning through the use of pleasure' (Sullivan 2003:155), which briefly functions to 'shatter identity, and dissolve the subject', in opposition to the way in which heteronomative sex reproduces selves and reaffirms fixed sexual categorisations (Halperin 1995:95). Terms in common usage in BDSM communities such as 'play' and 'scene' (referring to BDSM acts and the space entered in order to perform such acts) underline an explicitness about the theatricality of BDSM sexuality. The latter, like other 'queernesses', can serve to dissolve both narratives of the 'naturalness' of sexual orientation and action and the normative connections made between sexual acts and the stability of sexual identity/orientation/gender. In this analysis, some forms of BDSM behaviour can be seen as supportive of a notion of gender as performative, that is as highlighting the instability of heteronormative behaviours by staged mimicry (Butler 1991). Further, such terms support a notion of queer as both a set of practices and as an alternative position 'to the side' of homo and heteronormativity rather than opposed to it (Sedgwick 2003). Practitioners of BDSM commonly use terms such as 'pervert' to self-identify, as a category, which sits alongside and modifies other sexual labels such as heterosexual, homosexual, bisexual and queer.

Other theorists, however, have critiqued the position that BDSM is automatically a queer and politically powerful activity that challenges the naturalness and normality of heteronormative sex, fixed gendered and self identities. Authors such as Jeffreys (1996:86) maintain that BDSM 'eroticises the crude power difference of gender which fuels heterosexual desire, reinforcing rather than ending it'. Many BDSMers are uncomfortable with activities which seem more clearly perpetuating of traditional gender dynamics (e.g. 24/7 slavery, rape and domestic violence scenes), despite their overall emphasis on clear distinctions between fantasy and reality in BDSM play (Ritchie and Barker 2005). Sullivan (2003) argues that even practices that reverse such dynamics could be seen as perpetuating the dichotomies they may claim to challenge. Jeffreys sees BDSM as a form of internalised abuse (1996) against an inner self, and Sullivan's (2003) analysis of BDSM narratives reproduced in television programmes and books finds several examples of accounts of BDSM as an expression of a core, unified self, suggesting that BDSMers certainly do not all adhere to a queer agenda.

Arguments from BDSM organisations and communities against dominant negative understandings and treatment often involve reversing the claims that are made against them. The BDSM slogan 'Safe, Sane, Consensual' (SSC) explicitly counters popular taken-for-granted assumptions that BDSM activities are dangerous, mentally unhealthy and abusive (Langdridge and Butt 2005) as do more recent narratives of BDSM as 'healing' or 'therapeutic' (Barker, Iantaffi and Gupta in press). However, such norms within BDSM communities could be seen as shoring up problematic constructions of 'mental health versus illness' and liberal discourses around informed consent, as well as policing boundaries against certain forms of potentially transgressive behaviour while embracing others (e.g. see Downing in press). Langdridge and Butt (2004, 2005) found that BDSMers also often present their practice as involving 'power exchange', downplaying the sexual element and links between sex, violence and pain. They suggest that this could be due to attempts to present BDSM in acceptable ways, which could help gain them recognition as sexual citizens. Some have responded to these issues by proposing the slogan 'Risk Aware Consensual Kink' (RACK), as an alternative to 'Safe, Sane, Consensual' (Medlin 2001). This slogan makes it easier to bracket BDSM with dangerous sports rather than with pyschopathologies, allowing for a complexity of possible harmful behaviours. It also refuses what is seen by some as an unrealistic commitment to safety over risk-taking and instead puts in its place a sense of adult awareness of potential risk accompanied by harm reduction strategies.

BDSMers often defend their practices by drawing on narratives of 'free choice'. They emphasise the agency of the bottom in choosing to be topped, and also the seemingly paradoxical aspect that they are the one in the position of power (Ritchie and Barker 2005). Sullivan (2003), however, argues that this distancing of bottoms from 'real' submissiveness may serve to reaffirm heteronormativity by reproducing, rather than critiquing, culturally dominant associations between submissiveness, passivity, femininity and inferiority. Some feminists have argued that the notion of consent has often been used to justify women's inequality (Butler 1982). It could, however, be argued that any group in our society is unlikely to be able to entirely escape gendered power imbalances.

There are also problems with representations of BDSMers as a homogenous group with similar practices and reasons for such practices. BDSMers engage in a diversity of activities with motivations varying between people and within the same person on different occasions.[7] There are many styles and cultures under the umbrella of BDSM, much as with other sexualities, and differences between, for example, different generations of BDSMers, or lesbian, bisexual, trans, gay, queer and straight-identified scenes may be very significant. Hart (1998) avoids claiming that BDSM itself is queer but emphasises queer potentials in BDSM practices and the construction of BDSM identities. We feel that it is useful to consider the queerness of BDSM in understanding why it might be so threatening to some counsellors and psychotherapists but emphasise that individual clients presenting with BDSM behaviours will most likely span a vast spectrum of degree of identification with queer from complete rejection to acceptance, or regarding queer as one of the labels that they use for themselves and/or others.

Dominant discourses of BDSM and negative client experiences

Most texts and training courses for counsellors and psychotherapists, even those on sexualities, fail to mention BDSM at all. One of the authors of this chapter (Barker), when starting a sex therapy placement, accessed a very recent basic text aimed at informing counsellors and therapists about such issues. Hudson-Allez' (2005) *Sex and Sexuality: Questions and Answers for Counsellors and Psychotherapists* acknowledges that counsellors should only focus on 'resolving the behaviour' of BDSM clients if asked to by the client themselves, as they may not have a problem with it (p. 120). However, the book also reproduces many dominant discourses[8] about BDSM, which authors such as Kolmes, Stock and Moser (2006:314) have found contribute markedly to commonplace negative experiences of BDSM clients in therapy. Kolmes, Stock and Moser point out that therapists reproducing these discourses may prevent clients from coming out, or discourage them from returning to counselling if they have used their disclosure of BDSM as a 'screening process'. Kolmes, Stock and Moser (p. 318) report that bad experiences lead to some clients avoiding therapy for fear of it being repeated and others trying to suppress their BDSM desires having been treated by therapists who believed that they were 'sick'.

Dominant discourses which are frequently reproduced will now be outlined and exemplifed with quotes from Hudson-Allez' book (in italics). They will be briefly countered in relation to other evidence and considered in relation to the negative experiences of clients in Kolmes, Stock and Moser's research. A summary box of all the major assumptions and challenges will be provided at the end of this section.

'Why do some people enjoy the pain aspects, where as for others any sort of pain or discomfort is a complete turn off?' (p. 120)

This question reproduces the common discourse that BDSM is all about 'pain'. As mentioned before, several aspects (for example bondage, dominance and submission) may not even be about physical stimulation, and many BDSMers emphasise the role of power or pleasure over pain in their activities (Langdridge and Butt 2005). Physical stimulation can be regarded as a continuum, which differs for different people and at different times. Nichols (2006) suggests: 'think "pain" as in biting your lover in a moment of sexual abandon – not "pain" as in root canal' (p. 284). Some may enjoy extreme levels of pain for various reasons, but this could be seen as analogous to the pain experienced by long-distance runners or boxers in pursuit of their sport.

'An ideal dynamic might therefore be a sadomasochistic couple, where one partner enjoys giving the pain and humiliation that the other enjoys' (p. 119)

This statement privileges BDSM conducted within the context of a coupled relationship. It also suggests a norm of rigid top/bottom roles whereas many BDSMers regard themselves as 'switches' to some degree (enjoying both roles). The terms 'pain and humiliation' here may also obscure the fact that scenes are often, at least to some extent, orchestrated by the bottom with the top reading the bottom's state and doing things they know them to find fulfilling. Participants in Ritchie and Barker's (2005) research emphasised the prior negotiation of BDSM scenes to accommodate the desire of all involved, one concluding that 'everybody knows the bottom really runs the scene' (p. 233).

'Such behaviour is thought to be underpinned by severe childhood punishment that has become eroticised' (p. 119) *'the lovemap of a person's sexuality [. . .] has been vandalized by actual or vicarious abusive practices' (p. 120)*

This is a particularly concerning discourse presented, as it is, as factual information. Moser (2002) reports that there is no evidence that the incidence of childhood abuse is any different within and outside BDSM communities. Nordling, Sandabba, Santilla and Alison's extensive (2006) study found no differences in childhood attachment styles between BDSMers and others, refuting the notion that childhood experiences have 'vandalised' the development of a BDSM person's sexuality.

Such a discourse also clearly implies that BDSM is abnormal and unhealthy, as it is only apparent in those with 'damaged' upbringings. Kolmes, Stock and Moser (2006) found that such discourses are commonly reproduced in psychotherapy. Three major examples of biased, inadequate or inappropriate care listed by BDSM clients are: 'considering BDSM to be unhealthy', 'confusing BDSM with abuse', and 'assuming that BDSM interests are indicative of past family/spousal abuse' (p. 314). Particularly harmful were times when therapists assume that '"bottoms" are self-destructive' and/ or that 'past trauma is the cause of the BDSM interests' (p. 316).

'The client may present with "Monday morning rebound syndrome", which is when feelings of fear, disgust, self-loathing or remorse emerge hours or days after engaging in S and M activities, in which case the client may ask for help in stopping' (p. 120)

None of the authors of this chapter have ever come across 'Monday morning rebound syndrome' in our fairly extensive experience of various BDSM communities in both the UK and US. This discourse seems to make an implicit link between BDSM and drug use (the idea of a 'come down'), which could serve to further demonise and pathologise BDSM (by linking it to both an illegal activity and to addiction). Nichols (2006) reports that another common discourse around BDSM as addiction is that practices will escalate and become more extreme (the 'slippery slope' argument) and reports that there is no evidence of this, with most people 'levelling off' after their initial experiences in BDSM, although this level may vary between people.

The issues around clients being encouraged to stop BDSM must also be considered very carefully. Kolmes, Stock and Moser (2006:315) give examples where clients had been told by therapists to stop their BDSM practices. In one case the therapist told the client that she would not see her unless she stopped because BDSM is always abuse. In another case the therapist said she believed that BDSM was 'aberrant and harmful to people who practise it'. Kolmes, Stock and Moser say that the problematic nature of such scenarios can be clearly seen if compared to the hypothetical example of a counsellor telling a client to stop kissing or having sexual relationships with her husband in order to continue treatment. Nichols (2006) suggests a need for caution in dealing with clients who report wanting to stop BDSM themselves. She points out that the most common kinds of BDSM clients are likely to be 'newbies' (those just coming out) and, since they have grown up in a culture dominated by negative discourses around BDSM, they may well express shame and fear. Comparisons with the 'pink therapy' literature on dealing with LGB clients within a homophobic and biphobic society may be useful here (Neal and Davies 2000).

'Sadists may present with difficulties of hyposexuality, retarded ejaculation or erectile failure. Similarly, masochists may present with premature ejaculation and loss of libido as the behaviour becomes desensitised' (p. 120)

The notion of desensitisation is again suggestive of an addiction discourse, which pathologises BDSM. Also there are embedded assumptions here of BDSM as a particularly male practice, and one which is inevitably tied to heterosexual sex (with erection and penetration a necessary part of contact). For some, BDSM is a sexual activity, for others, it is entirely distinct from sex. Some people always have an orgasm during a BDSM scene, others do not even become sexually aroused. Some people need all sex to involve an element of BDSM play, others like to also have vanilla sex. Some will differ on the extent to which BDSM is sexual at different times and within different practices.

'The counsellor must be alert to whether the behaviour presented is associated with an antisocial personality disorder . . . there is a temporal coupling of erotic stimulation and violence in the childhood histories of all sexually psychopathic serial murders. . . . Therefore, for personal safety and the safety of others, a forensic referral in these cases might be thought to be essential.' (p. 120)

This statement reproduces the 'slippery slope' discourse highlighted above as well as putting consensual BDSM in the same category as rape and murder by suggesting that BDSMers and serial killers have the same linking of eroticism and violence in their developmental histories. Serial killers are a convenient current cultural bogeyman, omnipresent in media depictions and extremely rare in reality (Harrower 1998) and warnings relating to them represent unnecessary fear-mongering. Clearly BDSM relationships can become abusive, as can non-BDSM relationships, but the emphasis on safety in this quote suggests that this is more of a concern in the former case without providing evidence to support this. Confidentiality is a key area here as Kolmes, Stock and Moser (2006:316) report that BDSM clients are particularly concerned about counsellors 'making reports/breaking confidentiality because the therapist assumes others are at risk solely due to BDSM activities'.

Common assumptions about BDSM and challenges to those based on research in this area:

Underlying assumption about BDSM	Challenges to dominant discourses
BDSM is all about pain.	There may not be any pain involved. There are different kinds of pain.
BDSM always takes place in couple relationships.	Single people and those with multiple partners also engage in BDSM. It may not occur within the context of an ongoing relationship.
BDSMers always assume fixed roles (top or bottom; dom or sub).	Many people switch roles within and/or between scenes.
The top/dom has all the control.	Bottoms/subs are often perceived as having more control and negotiations usually take place in any case.

People who engage in BDSM have been abused or somehow damaged in their lives.	There is no evidence that the incidence of abuse is any greater amongst BDSMers than the general population.
BDSM is addictive and the start of a slippery slope into more extreme activities.	There is no evidence that BDSM is any more addictive than any other behaviour. Many experience an ebb and flow in their levels of BDSM activities and desire.
BDSM is always about sex.	BDSM may or may not take place in a sexual context/relationship.
BDSM is on the same continuum of behaviour as violent sadism and serial murder.	BDSM relationships are no more likely to be abusive than any other. There is generally a strong emphasis on consent and safety in BDSM relationships, communities and literature.

The negative experiences of BDSM clients reported here suggest a strong need for increasing BDSM awareness amongst therapists and counsellors, challenging their own belief systems around sexuality and encouraging exploration of dominant cultural discourses. Barker (2005) presents an example exercise, which aims to challenge counsellors' concerns about BDSM practices and acceptance of analogous culturally acceptable behaviours. Another important issue is therapists' knowledge: Kolmes, Stock and Moser (2006) found that many BDSM clients were frustrated by having to educate their therapists about BDSM, often in order to counter the dominant discourses highlighted above. One said she had to educate her therapist 'that it was not abuse, that it was not harmful to me, that I was not self sabotaging with it, nor acting out past family/spousal abuse. It actually took quite a few sessions to get the therapist over their hang-ups and misconceptions about BDSM. Time that could (have) been better spent on the actual issues I was there for' (p. 315). The issues of how counsellors and therapists can reflect on their own assumptions and enhance their understanding of BDSM are returned to in our consideration of good practice next.

Positive experiences and good practice with BDSM clients

So far, we have highlighted some of the challenges posed by dominant discourses on sexualities for kinky clients seeking therapeutic support.

However, Kolmes, Stock and Moser (2006:317) also report a number of examples of good practice, which they obtained from their previously mentioned survey of BDSM clients in psychotherapy. Major themes included:

(1) therapist(s) being open to reading/learning more about BDSM,
(2) therapist(s) showing comfort in talking about BDSM issues, and
(3) therapists who understand and promote 'safe, sane, consensual' BDSM.

Of course, this does not mean that all BDSM clients need to seek therapists specialising in BDSM issues, especially since they might be seeking therapy in relation to other aspects of their life. Nevertheless, being able to engage in a therapeutic relationship with a kink-friendly practitioner would mean that clients can be more relaxed and do not need to censor or edit themselves during sessions. Kink-friendly therapists display a whole list of character-istics, as highlighted by Kolmes, Stock and Moser (2006:317), such as 'being willing to raise questions about BDSM, normalising BDSM interests for clients new to BDSM, open-minded acceptance, being well informed about BDSM and the subculture (or even identifying as one who engages in BDSM practices), and not focusing on kinky behaviour when it's not the client's focus of treatment'. It is clear from this list that such a definition of a kink-friendly therapist could be equally applied to any other context, such as bisexuality or race. Therefore, it seems that we could define a kink-friendly mental health practitioner as someone who is willing to engage with the issue of BDSM not as a pathology but as a different cultural context, which may, or may not, be already familiar to them.

Both Bridoux (2000) and Nichols (2006) also suggest ways in which therapists can engage positively with BDSMers as clients. The former states that 'as therapists our duty is to leave our model of the world on the back burner, so that it doesn't interfere with the client's' (Bridoux 2000:30). In order to do this, he suggests the values of respect, relevance and ecology. That is we should consider how the issue of BDSM relates to the other aspects of the client's life and their larger systems. Much as these values are useful to bear in mind, we would like to argue that they are not as unproblematic as they might seem at first reading. Bridoux's statement about the necessity for therapists to put aside their own 'model of the world', for example, can be seen as unattainable from a social construc-tionist viewpoint. If we believe that our therapeutic actions and con-versations are joint ones, and that we can only know and act from our embodied positions, both as a client and therapist (Shotter 1993), then we can never put aside our model of the world since it is not separate from us. However, this does not mean justifying bigotry or moral relativism. On the contrary, such a position requires us, as therapists, to continuously engage with our own beliefs, stories and experiences as they form part of the negotiated understandings that we often form in therapy and that are themselves moral forms of social action (Gergen 2003).

From this standpoint, Nichols' (2006:286) suggestions for good practice are also valuable, yet not completely relevant to anyone operating from outside a psychodynamic model, which uses concepts such as countertransference. Nevertheless, she highlights the need for therapists working with kinky clients to deal 'with their own judgements, feelings and reactions to this sexual behavior' (ibid.) We would like to argue that a broader concept, which also invites therapists to engage with these issues, is that of reflexivity, as discussed next.

Working from a systemic and constructionist approach to therapy, Cecchin, Lane and Ray (1994:8) described the therapeutic process as happening 'in the interplay of the prejudices of therapist and client – a cybernetics of prejudice'. Prejudice, in this framework, can be defined as all that we (clients and therapists) bring with us to the therapy room. In this context, the therapy room 'reflects back only what is voiced within it' (Hare-Mustin 1997:557), with the potential of becoming a 'mirrored room' of society and its dominant discourses. Curiosity (Cecchin 1987), in this context, is an essential stance for the therapist who then does not become attached to one particular story or interpretation of meaning. This stance is just as essential for therapists to adopt when looking at themselves, as well as clients. Curiosity turned inwards, towards our own beliefs, stories, feelings and thoughts (that is our prejudices as here defined) can be defined as reflexivity.

Being reflexive when engaging BDSMers as clients in therapy can be seen as even more essential since talking about power is something that cannot be avoided when discussing BDSM. This can create an interesting context since power can be seen as a complex issue in therapy. After all, often the therapeutic encounter entails meeting in a safe space, in a ritualised manner, within clear and set boundaries and adopting particular roles (therapist/client), which have their own set of rules, responsibilities and obligations. Encountering BDSM in the therapy room requires therapists to engage seriously with the reflexive process in order to explore their own construct of power, pleasure and pain in relation to sexuality. In our opinion, this does not mean necessarily being comfortable with every BDSM practice that clients might talk about but rather to be conscious of one's levels of comfort around such issues, including practices and ideas that might 'squick'[9] us. If therapy is seen as a process that is co-created (Shotter and Katz 1998), then reflexivity is the ability that allows us, as therapists, to remain conscious co-creators throughout this process.

Looking at therapy as a 'cybernetics of prejudice' (Cecchin, Lane and Ray 1994), therefore, challenges traditional notions of neutrality in favour of reflexive practices and curiosity. Such reflexive practices can be seen not just as individual but also as relational. Relational reflexivity (Burnham

2005), in fact, could be seen as curiosity towards the process, rather than the content of therapy, allowing us to have meta-conversation with our clients: that is to talk about talking. Adopting a stance of relational-, as well as self-, reflexivity in therapy with kinky clients, might lead the therapist to ask questions such as: 'Is this conversation useful for you?', 'Are there books/leaflets/web sites, which you would like me to read so that I don't need to ask you basic questions about your BDSM practices?', 'I notice that you waited five sessions before mentioning BDSM. Was this because it was not relevant until now or was this due to something else?' Engaging in meta-conversations with clients might hopefully avoid some of the negative experiences encountered by BDSMers in therapy, as described earlier, since clients would have an opportunity to address openly something that could easily become a taboo subject.

We would like to argue that engaging seriously with personal and relational reflexivity could be a 'force for change' (Leppington 1991) for therapeutic practices with kinky clients and one that is applicable across a wide range of approaches to therapy. However, reflexivity also invites us to view the therapeutic process as circular rather than linear, as something that is co-created by therapist and client and, as such, situated within both the dominant and counter-dominant discourses that are embodied by them. When linear understandings of cause and effect and notions of immutable truths, such as what constitutes consent in a sexual encounter, are put into question as contested, co-created and embodied notions, there can be a sense of crisis or lack of points of references. One of the authors (Iantaffi) has found the concept of irreverence to be a useful foundation from which to know and act as a therapist. Irreverence is defined by Cecchin, Lane and Ray (1992:11) as 'to never accept one logical level of a position but, rather, to play with varying levels of abstractions, changing from one level to another. Instead of accepting any fixed descriptions, irreverence posits eroding certainty'. We would argue that the erosion of certainty within therapy could create new spaces in which to talk about queer sexualities, including BDSM, in non-pathologising ways.

Conclusions

In this chapter, we have addressed BDSM both in the context of queer sexualities and therapeutic practices. We have highlighted how the relationship between kinky clients and therapy is not always an easy one, since BDSM is often still seen as pathological. We have also discussed some of the dominant discourses about BDSM and mental health, as well as negative experiences of therapy for clients who engage in BDSM practices. Some tools for good practice were also introduced, although we are aware that these could be seen as just an initial step and that further dialogue is needed.

Kolmes, Stock and Moser (2006:306) state that 'until BDSM practices and lifestyles are included routinely as part of the human sexuality component of training for all practitioners, and until the mental health profession begins to recognise BDSM individuals as a subculture requiring special knowledge, skills, and sensitivity, there remains the risk that therapists may be providing services to BDSM individuals without ever having received appropriate study, training, or supervision'. They also emphasise that it is important that therapists do not present themselves as BDSM-positive when they are not actually knowledgeable as many clients experienced this as problematic in their survey.

In this context, it is also worth reflecting on the foundation of our therapeutic practices, that is the theoretical approach underpinning our actions and conversations. It could indeed be argued that some approaches to therapy would not be as pathologising as others in relation to BDSM. It is then vital to query not just our technique and methods, when reflecting on our therapeutic practices with kinky clients, but also our theoretical orientation, to see whether coherence is possible across these dimensions. In our experience, BDSM is not yet routinely discussed or included in the syllabus for trainee therapists and both tutors and clinical supervisors have often not yet addressed their own prejudices towards BDSM practices. Nevertheless, the professional landscape is starting to shift and kink-aware professionals are becoming more visible, thanks also to the internet (e.g. Kink Aware Professionals 2006), and to the slowly growing body of literature on the subject. Challenging dominant discourses about BDSM is not always easy, as all three of us know from experience, but less traditional approaches to therapy (e.g. constructionism, narrative therapy, existential therapy) are opening new and wider arenas in which these debates can take place.

Notes

1 There are also a number of other terms for practice and identity that are used, often for contextual reasons of difference in region, era, cultural formation and/or sexual community. Such labels include 'kink' and 'leather' or 'leathersex'. For simplicity, we have used the term 'BDSMer' here to refer to those involved in BDSM communities or practices in whatever way.
2 *R v. Brown* [1994] 1 AC 212.
3 Various words are used for the different participants or positions in BDSM. Here we use 'top' for a person in the position of power or giving out the stimulation and 'bottom' for a person who opts to give over power or control of the scene. A 'switch' is someone who takes both kinds of roles (see Easton and Hardy 2001, 2003).
4 They are also classified as disorders in the F65 section of the international World Health Organization *International Classification of Diseases* (ICD) (Reiersøl and Skeid 2006).
5 It is notable that queer theory, emerging as it does from deconstructionist

practice, provides one of the most useful frameworks for non-pathologising discussion of BDSM. This is indicative of a cultural shift away from the modernist validation of bodies, narratives and identities as singular monolithic concepts. In twenty-first century Western culture there is a wider acceptance of, and need for, descriptors that allow for contradiction and disparity, refusing notions of inherent value. There is much to be said on this topic, but it is beyond the scope of the current chapter to examine this turn in detail.

6 'Vanilla' is a term used, mostly in BDSM communities, to refer to non-BDSM sex.

7 For example, being the submissive party in an SM scene may allow someone to safely relinquish the responsibilities of day-to-day adult life, to gain control in one specified area as they negotiate the scene, to increase their sense of intimacy with the others involved, to break taboos, to prove their ability to endure what is happening to them, to enjoy a pleasurable physical sensation and/or to induce a meditative state.

8 By 'dominant discourse' we mean the prevailing cultural understandings which are reproduced and legitimated in everyday talk, mass media representations and so on (Van Dijk 1993).

9 Nichols (2006:288) presents an interesting exploration of the BDSM term 'squick' as a useful concept. It can be defined as a strong negative emotional reaction to an activity which acknowledges that 'you do not actually judge the activity as wrong or bad'.

References

APA DSM-IV-TR (text revision) (2000) [Online] www.behavenet.com/capsules/disorders [accessed May 2007].

Baggaley, M. (2006) Is an interest in BDSM a pathological disorder or a normal variant of human sexual behaviour? *Lesbian & Gay Psychology Review*, **6**, 253–4.

Barker, M. (2003) Rewriting the sexual script? Constructions of sexuality in the bi, poly and S/M communities. Presentation to the fifteenth annual international congress on Personal Construct Psychology, Huddersfield, July 2003.

Barker, M. (2005) Experience of SM awareness training. *Lesbian & Gay Psychology Review*, **6**, 268–73.

Barker, M., Iantaffi, A. and Gupta, C (in press) The power of play: healing narratives in BDSM. In D. Langdridge and M. Barker (eds), *Safe, Sane and Consensual: Contemporary Perspectives on Sadomasochism*. London: Palgrave.

Beckmann, A. (2001) Deconstructing myths: the social construction of 'sadomasochism' versus 'subjugated knowledges' of practitioners of consensual 'SM'. *Journal of Criminal Justice and Popular Culture*, **8**, 66–95.

Bridoux, D. (2000) Kink therapy: SM and sexual minorities. In C. Neal and D. Davies (eds), *Pink Therapy 3: Issues in Therapy with Lesbian, Gay, Bisexual and Transgender Clients*. Buckingham: Open University Press, pp. 22–34.

Burnham, J. (2005) Relational reflexivity: a tool for socially constructing therapeutic relationships. In C. Flaskas, B. Mason and A. Perlesz (eds), *The Space Between: Experience, Context and Process in the Therapeutic Relationship*. London: Karnac Books, pp. 95–110.

Butler, J. (1982) Lesbian S&M: the politics of dis-illusion. In R.R. Linden, D.R. Pagano, D.E.H. Russell and S.L. Star (eds), *Against Sadomasochism: A Radical Feminist Analysis*. San Francisco: Frog in the Well, pp. 168–75.

Butler, J. (1991) Imitation and gender insubordination. In D. Fuss (ed.), *Inside/Out: Lesbian Theories, Gay Theories*. New York: Routledge, pp. 13–31.

Califia, P. (1980) Feminism and sadomasochism. In P. Califia (2000) *Public Sex: The Culture of Radical Sex*. San Francisco, CA: Cleis Press, pp. 168–80.

Cecchin, G. (1987) Hypothesizing, circularity, and neutrality revisited: an invitation to curiosity. *Family Process*, **26**, 405–13.

Cecchin, G., Lane, G. and Ray, W.A. (1992) *Irreverence: A Strategy for Therapists' Survival*. London: Karnac Books.

Cecchin, G., Lane, G. and Ray, W.A. (1994) *The Cybernetics of Prejudices in the Practice of Psychotherapy*. London: Karnac Books.

Chaline, E. (2005) Spanner: S/M, consent and the law in the UK. *Lesbian & Gay Psychology Review*, **6**, 283–7.

Denman, C. (2004) *Sexuality: A Biopsychosocial Approach*. London: Palgrave.

Downing, L. (in press) Beyond safety: erotic asphyxiation and the limits of S/M discourse. In D. Langdridge and M. Barker (eds), *Safe, Sane and Consensual: Contemporary Perspectives on Sadomasochism*. London: Palgrave.

Easton, D. and Hardy, J.W. (2001) *The New Bottoming Book*. California: Greenery Press.

Easton, D. and Hardy, J.W. (2003) *The New Topping Book*. California: Greenery Press.

Freud, S. (1905) Three Essays on the Theory of Sexuality. In J. Strachey (ed.) (1953–74), *The Standard Edition of the Complete Psychological Works of Sigmund Freud*. London: Hogarth Press.

Gergen, K.J. (2003) Knowledge as socially constructed. In M. Gergen and K.J. Gergen (eds), *Social Construction: A Reader*. London: Sage Publications, pp. 15–17.

Gosselin, C. and Wilson, G. (1980) *Sexual Variations: Fetishism, Sadomasochism and Transvestism*. London: Faber and Faber.

Halperin, D.M. (1995) *Saint Foucault: Towards a Gay Hagiography*. New York: Oxford University Press.

Hare-Mustin, R.T. (1997) Discourse in the mirrored room: a post-modern analysis of therapy. In M.M. Gergen and S.N. Davis (eds), *Toward a New Psychology of Gender: A Reader*. London: Routledge, pp. 553–74.

Harrower, J. (1998) *Applying Psychology to Crime*. London: Hodder and Stoughton.

Hart, L. (1998) *Between the Body and the Flesh*. New York: Columbia University Press.

Hudson-Allez, G. (2005) *Sex and Sexuality: Questions and Answers for Counsellors and Therapists*. London: Whurr Publishers.

Informed Consent (2006) [Online] www.informedconsent.co.uk/ [accessed May 2006].

Janus, S.S. and Janus, C.L. (1994) *Janus Report on Sexual Behavior*. Chichester: John Wiley.

Jeffreys, S. (1996) Heterosexuality and the desire for gender. In D. Richardson (ed.), *Theorising Heterosexuality*. Buckingham: Open University Press, pp. 75–90.

Kink-Aware Professionals (2006) [Online] www.ncsfreedom.org/kap [accessed May 2007].

Kleinplatz, P. and Moser, C. (2005) Is S/M pathological? *Lesbian & Gay Psychology Review*, **6**, 255–60.

Kleinplatz, P. and Moser, C. (eds) (2006) *SM: Powerful Pleasures*. Binghamton, NY: Haworth Press.

Kolmes, K., Stock, W. and Moser, C. (2006) Investigating bias in psychotherapy with BDSM clients. In P. Kleinplatz and C. Moser (eds), *SM: Powerful Pleasures*. Binghamton, NY: Haworth Press, pp. 301–24.

Kutchins, H. and Kirk, S.A. (1997) *Making Us Crazy: DSM: The Psychiatric Bible and the Creation of Mental Disorders*. London: Constable.

Langdridge, D. and Barker, M. (eds) (in press) *Safe, Sane and Consensual: Contemporary Perspectives on Sadomasochism*. London: Palgrave.

Langdridge, D. and Butt, T.W. (2004) A hermeneutic phenomenological investigation of the construction of sadomasochistic identities. *Sexualities*, **7**, 31–53.

Langdridge, D. and Butt, T. (2005) The erotic construction of power exchange. *Journal of Constructivist Psychology*, **18**, 65–74.

Leppington, R. (1991) From constructivism to social constructionism and doing critical therapy. *Human Systems*, **2**, 79–103.

Macey, D. (1993) *The Lives of Michel Foucault*. London: Hutchinson.

Medlin, J. (2001) SSC vs. RACK. [Online] www.leathernroses.com/generalbdsm/medlinssc.htm [accessed May 2007].

Moser, C. (2002) What do we really know about S/M: myths and realities. Paper presented at the 34th conference of the *American Association of Sex Educators, Counselors, and Therapists*, Miami.

Moser, C. and Levit, E.E. (1987) An explanatory-descriptive study of a sado-masochistically oriented sample. *The Journal of Sex Research*, **23**, 322–37.

Neal, C. and Davies, D. (eds) (2000) *Pink Therapy 3: Issues in Therapy with Lesbian, Gay, Bisexual and Transgender Clients*. Buckingham: Open University Press.

Nichols, M. (2006) Psychotherapeutic issues with 'kinky' clients: clinical problems, yours and theirs. In P. Kleinplatz and C. Moser (eds), *SM: Powerful Pleasures*. Binghamton, NY: Haworth Press, pp. 281–300.

Nordling, N., Sandabba, N.K., Santilla, P. and Alison, L. (2006) Differences and similarities between gay and straight individuals involved in the sadomasochistic subculture. In P. Kleinplatz and C. Moser (eds), *SM: Powerful Pleasures*. Binghamton, NY: Haworth Press, pp. 41–58.

Plummer, K. (1995) *Telling sexual stories: Power, change and social worlds*. London: Routledge.

Reiersøl, O. and Skeid, S. (2006) The ICD diagnoses of fetishism and SM. In P. Kleinplatz and C. Moser (eds), *SM: Powerful Pleasures*. Binghamton, NY: Haworth Press, pp. 243–62.

Ridinger, R.B. (2006) Negotiating limits: the legal status of S/M in the United States. In P. Kleinplatz and C. Moser (eds), *SM: Powerful Pleasures*. Binghamton, NY: Haworth Press, pp. 189–216.

Ritchie, A. and Barker, M. (2005) Feminist SM: a contradiction in terms or a way of challenging traditional gendered dynamics through sexual practice? *Lesbian & Gay Psychology Review*, **6**, 227–39.

Rubin, G. (1984) Thinking sex: notes for a radical theory on the politics of sexuality.

In C. Vance (ed.), *Pleasure and Danger: Exploring Female Sexuality*. London: Routledge, pp. 267–319.

Scarlet Magazine (2006) Should you make your fantasies come true? *Scarlet*, July, 2005, 30–4.

Sedgwick, E. (2003) *Touching Feeling: Affect, Pedagogy, Performativity*. Durham: Duke University Press.

Shotter, J. (1993) *Conversational Realities*. London: Sage.

Shotter, J. and Katz, A.M. (1998) Creating relational realities: responsible responding to poetic 'movements' and 'moments'. In S. McNamee and K.J. Gergen (eds), *Relational Responsibility: Resources for Sustainable Dialogue*. London: Sage, pp. 151–61.

Sisson, K. (2005) The cultural formation of S/M: history and analysis. *Lesbian & Gay Psychology Review*, **6**, 147–62.

Storr, M. (2003) *Latex and Lingerie: Shopping for Pleasure at Ann Summers Parties (Materiali-Zing Culture)*. Oxford: Berg.

Sue, D., Sue, D.W. and Sue, S. (2000) *Understanding Abnormal Behaviour*. Boston: Houghton Mifflin.

Sullivan, N. (2003) Sadomasochism as resistance? In N. Sullivan (ed.), *A Critical Introduction to Queer Theory*. Edinburgh: Edinburgh University Press, pp. 151–67.

Taylor, G.W. and Ussher, J.M. (2001) Making sense of S&M: a discourse analytic account. *Sexualities*, **4**, 293–314.

Toronto news (2004) www.xtra.ca/site/toronto2/VXnews/body5.shtm [accessed May 2004].

Van Dijk, T. (1993) Principles of critical discourse analysis. *Discourse and Society*, **4**, 249–83.

Weiss, M. (2006) Mainstreaming kink: the politics of BDSM representations in U.S. popular media. In P. Kleinplatz and C. Moser (eds), *SM: Powerful Pleasures*. Binghamton, NY: Haworth Press, pp. 103–32.

Wiseman, J. (1996) *SM 101: A Realistic Introduction*. San Francisco: Greenery Press.

Chapter 9

Queer methodologies

Peter Hegarty

In some very important ways, the task of writing a chapter on *queer methodologies* is doomed to failure; the two words of my title are reluctant bedfellows. Methodologies are logics that attempt the impossible task of arranging different ways of knowing into hierarchical orders, based on competing ethical, practical and epistemological values. While 'queer' is sometimes used as a supplementary term to 'lesbian, gay, bisexual and transgender', or as an overarching category that includes them all (and sometimes others), it is the understanding of 'queer' as an anti-essentialist counter-disciplinary project, committed to partiality and irony, that concerns me most here. *Queer* strives to trouble Enlightenment projects, including the fiction that the field of study known as 'methodology' is rational and coherent. As such, 'queer methodologies' might be contradictions in terms; the first term insists on pluralism, heterogeneity and understandings of difference that the second term writes off as error variance. Nor is it clear if a chapter on queer methodologies will review those that exist, or consider what queer methodologies of the future might be. When placed before 'methodology' is queer an adjective, a verb, or both?

This chapter can only be a partial account of these problems, and it will be informed by my involvement in the fields of social psychology and the history of psychology in particular. My focus is going to be on that 'workhorse of social psychological research, the experimental method' (Aronson, Wilson and Brewer 1998:100). Coming from LGBTQ psychology, experiments might seem like an odd place to site a queer project. Kitzinger (1997; see also Kitzinger and Coyle 2002) describe social constructionist and 'traditional' epistemologies (including experiments) in lesbian and gay psychology as engaged in politically related but epistemologically dissonant projects. Social constructionists critique the heteronormative, androcentric, imperialist edifice of psychology, while traditionalists use psychology's fact-producing methods in the service of securing civil rights and other benefits for lesbians and gay men. Quantitative methods are often described as useful to lesbian and gay psychology as means of debunking homophobic myths and 'bad science' (see Herek 1998) while qualitative methods are described as means of enacting more collaborative, and less hierarchical relationships with research subjects (Coyle 2000). Through careful and insightful readings of both homophobic and gay-affirmative quantitative research in psychology, Noam Warner (2004) reaches the conclusion that queer methodologies in psychology are necessarily qualitative methods.

This chapter gambles on the idea that an understanding of quantitative methods forgets much about the ways that these methods have been practised in the past, and encodes a limited imagination of what they might do in the future. I am going to celebrate the diversity of the queer weeds that grow in the cracks of laboratory knowledge which positivist narratives rarely cherish and social constructionist quantophobia neglects to nurture. This chapter is not an argument against qualitative methods throughout; its logic will be transparently indebted to thinking from the qualitative social sciences. Rather, it is an attempt to historicize experiments by animating the queer voices in the 'stubborn particulars' of social psychology (Cherry 1995) and to use those conversations across time to push past the hetero-normative and non-reflexive horizons that 'methodologies' so often create.

Experimental and queer subcultures

Psychology laboratories and queer subcultures have mutually defining histories. The professions of psychology and psychiatry expanded rapidly in the years after World War II, peopled often by veterans who received generous financial aid for university educations through the GI Bill[1] (Capshew 1999; Herman 1995). Post-war in the US, psychology labora-tories multiplied with generous contract support from funding agencies (Darley 1952) and appeared to some to afford a positivist vision of an experimental science of social relations (see Allport 1954). President Eisenhower described the Cold War as a psychological battle for the hearts and minds of Americans, making the psychological loyalty of individuals a matter of national security (see Lutz 1997). However, gay men and lesbians were on the wrong side of this state-sponsored war. Homosexuality was grounds for exclusion from military service for the first time in World War II. A range of ad hoc biological, psychiatric and psychological techniques were piloted as ways of detecting true homosexuals from heterosexual men who were feared to be 'malingering' as homosexual to escape active service (Berube 1990). Servicemen dismissed from the army with 'dishonourable discharges' for homosexuality were barred from the GI Bill that would have allowed them access to scientific training. Gay men and lesbians were further excluded from government work under a series of executive orders signed in the early 1950s that barred them from an ever-widening range of government positions. Ultimately, the FBI collaborated with local police forces to ensure that there were no 'sexual psychopaths' in government employment (see Terry 1999). 'Sexual psychopath' laws were exercised with more enthusiasm in the 1950s, leading many gay men and lesbians to have their first encounters with psychology through enforced psychiatric institutionalisation (Freedman 1987; Miller 2002). Enforcement of the military ban on homosexuality intensified after the war (Berube 1990). Some psychologists even tried to develop experimental technologies by which gay men could be detected and excluded from intelligence services (Gentile and Kinsman 2000).

This 'sex panic' (Rubin 1984) created a climate of extreme suspicion and subsequently had an impact on research on homosexuality in the emerging human, cognitive, behavioural and psychological sciences, which curtailed the kinds of knowledge that experimental researchers in these various disciplines could construct. In light of Kinsey's findings about the sexual practices of American women, the Reece Commission put pressure on the Rockefeller Foundation to withdraw their support for his Institute of Sex Research. Kinsey died, a broken and exhausted man only a few years later (Gathorne-Hardy 1998; Jones 1997). Evelyn Hooker, whose experimental work debunked much of the earlier wartime work on the 'homosexual personality' was scrutinised by her funders to make sure that she was not a lesbian (Hooker 1993). Astronomer Frank Kameny lost his job in a government laboratory and later became an activist who spearheaded the move to have homosexuality removed from the DSM^2 (Marcus 1992). This is not to say that lesbian and gay experimenters did not exist. Many gay professionals participated in underground networks such as those described by 'Dr. Anonymous' at the first meeting of the American Psychiatric Association in which openly gay and lesbian people spoke for themselves (Bayer 1981). Roger Brown's sexuality appears to have been an open secret (see Brown 1989). Daryl Bem told his wife Sandra that he was more attracted to men than to women on their first date, but the couple went on to lecture publicly about how to have an egalitarian heterosexual marriage in the early 1970s (Bem 1998).

In short, the closet was a card of entry into the experimental cultures of social psychology that developed in post-World War II America. The gay and lesbian subcultures that developed at this time ultimately gave rise to 'queer theory' (Minton 1997) but were deliberately expunged from the laboratories and university classrooms where psychology's expert discourse and methodological norms were taking shape. In spite of this, curious similarities between the two can be noted: in both spaces people explore new identities and push past the received wisdom of what 'the social' might become (Hegarty 2001). However, unlike psychology, queer subcultures are not invested with the authority of science. For example, within queer theory gender 'performances' appear as 'play acting' while the artifice of social psychological experiments, including those taking gender into account are based on exploring the 'reality' of human sociality. Small wonder that these two subcultures often reach radically different epistemological conclusions, for example about how gender might be known (see Parlee 1996).

Perhaps the most notorious social psychology experiment from this period is Stanley Milgram's experiment on obedience. Ostensibly unrelated to queer theory at all, I would like to argue that this experiment was compromised in its design and interpretation by Cold War sex panic. Most of us who have been indoctrinated by the received wisdom in social psychology know the story: Milgram's participants believed that they were following an experimenter's orders by administering painful, and ultimately lethal, electric shocks to strangers ('learners') as part of an experiment on learning. Participants delivered the electric shocks beyond the point where the 'learner' (actually a confederate) complained about his heart condition, banged on the wall, begged to be released from the experimental apparatus, and ultimately fell silent. Many psychologists found Milgram's experiments unbelievable, replicated his procedures, and observed similar results in their own studies (see Milgram 1974).

The received wisdom in the field is that Milgram's experiment evidences how obedience to authority can lead ordinary individuals to engage in surprisingly evil actions, and thus provides a potent explanation of ordinary Germans' participation in the Holocaust (see Bauman 1989; Brown 1986; Hogg and Vaughn 2005). This interpretation of the experiment has been problematised within psychology in two principal ways. First, Baumrind (1964) raised the question of the experiment's use of deception as harmful to both individual participants and the public image of science. A second concern is raised by the possibility that the participants knew the true purpose of the experiment, such that their behaviour in the laboratory is little more than assent to the experimenter's demand, rendering the experiment itself epistemologically void (see also Orne 1962). In other words, while some critics thought the experiment too realistic, others thought it not realistic enough.

Both of these critiques of the canonical reading of Milgram's experiment take on new meanings when we keep in mind the concerns of queer subjects that his own experimental subculture disavowed. First, consider the Milgram experiment as an analogue of the Holocaust. Queer people who are particularly vulnerable to state-sponsored violence (including that of the Nazis) have a particular stake in the production of this critical knowledge. However, in the narratives of the Holocaust to which Milgram's work refers, the persecution of gay men and lesbians is never explicitly mentioned. Indeed, in the early 1960s when Milgram's work was published, such claims would have been controversial. Nazi versions of Paragraph 175 had been suspended in East Germany in the late 1950s, but Paragraph 175 was used to convict over 3,000 men each year in West Germany in the early 1960s.[3] Laws against 'sexual psychopaths' were also enforced in many US jurisdictions. Remembering the lesbian and gay victims of the Holocaust would have required Milgram to query the sex laws of Western democracies of his time, a radical project with which his experiment failed to engage.

Next consider the claim that the participant in the experiment simply agrees to the experimenter's 'demands' and knows that the situation is so extreme that it cannot possibly be real. The 'cover story' for the Milgram experiment trades on the existence of, and public familiarity with, behaviourist psychology; the participant arrives at the laboratory armed with the knowledge that psychologists deliver electric shocks to people to make them learn new things. Not only was this believable in the early 1960s, but some of Milgram's participants may have been aware that such procedures were used to try to make gay and lesbian people 'learn' heterosexual responses. Reparative therapy uses electric shocks, delivered in response to arousal to homoerotic stimuli to make gay/lesbian people 'learn' to be straight.[4] Along with electroshock, castration, clitorectomy, lobotomy and arduous psychoanalysis it was part of the psychiatric arsenal used to extinguish homosexuality from American selves during the time of Milgram's experiments (Katz 1976). Similar procedures were used in UK psychiatry from the 1950s until the 1980s. Some psychologists who practised this work believed that they were helping unfortunate homosexuals to become better people. Others knew from the start that reparative therapy would be a failed project. Still others remind us of the shared history that queers have with Milgram when they recall that they were just obeying authority:

> Well I didn't have much choice. That was a clinical placement. I was [the consultant's] first student. Basically the first year I was there, more or less all I ever did was shove electricity down homosexual patients.
> cited in Bartlett, King and Smith (2004)

Finally, consider Baumrind's (1964) critique that the Milgram experiment is unethical for its use of deception methodologies, a criticism that Milgram countered with a follow-up questionnaire of participants showing that virtually all were unharmed by the experience, and supported the continuation of the experiment. Social psychology laboratories were not the only closed spaces in which people played with pain, obedience and power in the post-war era. During this period, autonomous SM cultures also developed in North America (Sisson 2005). In Milgram's writings the existence of SM provides a background hypothesis that is refuted in favour of his claim that 'evil' in the service of authority is a capacity of ordinary people:

> In the minds of some critics, there is an image of man (sic) that simply does not admit of the type of behaviour observed in the experiment. Ordinary people, they assert, do not administer painful shocks to a

protesting individual simply because they are ordered to do so. Only Nazis and sadists perform this way.

Milgram (1974:169)

Milgram here contributes to a long history of conflating the psychological motivations of sadomasochism (SM) and Nazi violence (see also Moore 2005); both are exceptional and beyond the explanation of the 'evil' actions of the ordinary people who find their way into Milgram's experiment. Social psychology experiments were later referenced in debates amongst feminists about sadomasochism. For example, Linden, in the introduction to *Against Sadomasochism: A Radical Feminist Analysis*, described the experience of sadists and masochists as akin to that of the prisoners and guards in Zimbardo's famous prison experiment[5] where 'guards' became habituated to sadistic (S) behaviour towards 'prisoners'. 'Just as the "guards" made an easy accommodation to wielding power, we can expect that sadists who regularly practice dominant roles would become habituated to sadism, perhaps failing to comprehend its extremity' (Linden 1982:8–9).

Yet, contrary to Linden's and Milgram's suggestion, the practice of sadism in SM cultures might have provided Zimbardo and Milgram with methodological resources that would have curtailed the unethical practices of their experiments. Here, I am referring to the practice of using agreed-upon signals, such as safety words, that allow the masochist (M) to limit the scope of SM play and consequently to enter into that play more fully, '[I]t is always important that the M be given an "out" . . . Regardless, if the S is worth his salt he will have made some provision for this' (Townsend 2000:131).

Had Milgram and Zimbardo found common kinship with such practices as the use of safety words, either in their construction or in their interpretation, their experiments might have created still bolder knowledge about the ethics of consent in situations structured by obedience, power and role-playing.

As it is, social psychologists have not solved the dilemma of how to do experiments without deception (Sieber, Iannuzzo and Rodriguez 1995). It remains an ordinary practice in their laboratories, and one that has costs for researchers as well as participants (see Oliansky 1991). In spite of these obvious problems in experimental culture, there is a failure to look at the kinds of practical knowledge developed in queer sites, such as SM sub-cultures, for ways of pushing beyond these dilemmas of consent, freedom, power and coercion.

How do you identify?

My discussion of the Milgram experiment presumes that there are multiple ways of writing about, and of remembering, what happens in experimental situations, and that queer methodologies might be practised through close attention to the implicit sexual politics involved in both concrete methodological practices and the general claims about human psychology that experiments warrant. Thus, it is hardly surprising that the reporting of experiments is highly codified, most obviously in the *Publication Manual of the American Psychological Association* (American Psychological Association 1994). Eager to distance itself from psychology's troubling homophobic past, the manual urges that 'people who are not heterosexual' should be described in published works as follows. 'The clearest way to refer inclusively to people whose orientation is not heterosexual is to write *lesbians, gay men*, and *bisexual women or men* – although somewhat long, the phrase is accurate' (p. 67).

This shift from medicalised terms to community-derived terms attempts to bring about a break with the stereotypes of the past. Yet, as Walsh-Bowers (1999) has noted, the *Publication Manual* proscribes particular ways of seeing the world. For example, by subdividing the 'method' section into a quite cursory 'participants' section, and more lengthy 'materials' and 'procedure' sections, the *Publication Manual* treats people as inert resources, much like the materials that appear in natural science laboratories.[6] As Walsh-Bowers (1999) notes, a natural science model of understanding that positions research participants as objects of knowledge who are separate and distant from the psychologists who study them is far from a neutral stance. By miming the forms of writing that have long been practised in the natural sciences, the *Publication Manual* not only proscribes a genre of writing but also denies that that genre is a genre. Since its inception in the seventeenth century, the scientific journal article has been promoted as a means of reporting 'matters of fact' that avoids 'meddling with Divinity, metaphysics, Morals, Politics, grammar, Rhetorick, or Logicks' (Hooke 1663, cited in Bernal 1965:455). As such it is one of the literary mediums through which scientists circulate an image of their activities operating in what Traweek (1988) calls a 'culture of no culture'.

Are there possibilities of queer knowledge that are suppressed by the codification of 'lesbians, gay men and bisexual women or men' as the accurate way or referring to 'people who are not heterosexual'? This question recalls Judith Butler's (1993) claim about identification that elaborates how, '[I]dentity categories tend to be instruments of regulatory regimes, whether as the normalizing categories of oppressive structures or as the rallying points for a liberatory contestation of that very oppression' (p. 308).

It is this opaqueness of identity categories that the *Publication Manual* wants to render transparent with the notion that there is a single accurate way to describe 'people who are not heterosexual'. However, such assumptions are challenged. Project Sigma's 2004 gay men's sex survey[7] is one of several annual surveys conducted 'to collect a limited amount of information from a substantial number of men' (Weatherburn, Reid, Hickson,

Hammond and Stevens 2004:2). More than 32,216 self-report question-naires were distributed to 113 HIV health promotion agencies in England, Wales and Scotland. The survey was also posted online in English and Spanish. Of the 19,210 surveys returned, 3,208 were excluded. Most exclusions occurred because the respondents were not resident in the UK, but 383 men were excluded because there was neither 'evidence of sex with men in the previous year or . . . gay, bisexual, or queer identity' (p. 4). In making this determination about identity, the researchers relied on the men's own words. These were introduced by an open-ended questionnaire item, 'What term do you usually use to describe yourself sexually?' While most respondents identified as gay (n = 13,030) or bisexual (n = 1961) in response to this question, 893 specified that they usually did not use a term. However, these terms failed to exhaust the diversity of identities that men used to describe themselves. Of the 92 men (0.6%) who ticked *other* and remained in the sample, 18 identified as 'queer', one as 'queer as fuck', eight identified as 'homosexual' one a 'homosexualist'. Five men identified as 'bi-curious', five were 'curious', including one that was 'curious, not hetero and not gay', and one that was 'still curious'. Five men identified as 'open minded', one simply 'open' and one 'open to offers'. Two identified as 'confused', including one that was 'confused and experimenting'. Four men identified as 'straight' and three as 'heterosexual' or 'hetero'. Two men identified as transgendered and three as transsexual (two male-to-female and one unspecified). One man identified as a 'transvestite'. One man each said: 'anything – whatever you want I got it'; 'batty boy'; 'batty'; 'bent'; 'bloke who likes having sex with men'; 'discreet' (sic); 'dilemma'; 'experimental'; 'free-spirited'; 'goth'; happy'; 'I am me – no pigeon holes'; 'I like both, but very picky'; 'lad who only fancies lads'; 'non-heterosexual'; 'not sure'; 'man who has sex with men'; 'proficient'; 'raving old poof'; 'sexually active'; 'trysexual – I'll try anything sexual'; 'unique'; 'wish to try other sex'; 'women alluring, men re-assuring' (p. 6). To my knowledge, Weatherburn, Reld, Hickson, Hammond and Stephens (2005) have not published their work in an *APA* journal or subjected it to that organisation's norms. I think that this is a very good thing, for in telling us more about these men's descriptions of themselves than the *APA* would advise, some horizons of quantitative research are visible in this report. When I read this list of terms some of them made me laugh because they seemed to subvert the question that the researchers asked. Others made me feel uncomfortable as they are terms I once used to describe myself but have long since given up. Collectively, they made me wonder when and where sincerity, irony, cooperation and dissent might be the intended effects of nominating the sexual self with a particular label. I was thrown back on the conclusion that it would be impossible to now know which motives lay behind the writing of particular terms.

In other words, by telling their readers more than the APA dutifully proscribe, Weatherburn, Reld, Hickson, Hammond and Stephens (2005) also provided us with the text that we need to recognise our ignorance about what 'people who are not heterosexual' are thinking when they give of their time, effort, and privacy to research. Nominations of one's identity, even those that appear on factual social science questionnaires, are never simply accounts of pre-existing identities; rather those identities are called into being through the act of naming itself. Such an identification is, in Butler's terms, 'a production, usually in response to a request'. 'Experimental' and 'free-spirited' may be obviously produced accounts of identity, but their reprinting here shows how the more quotidian 'gay' and 'bisexual' are productions also; sex with men, or with men and women is no guarantee that a man will identify as 'gay' or 'bisexual'.

Finally, this list shows the impossibility of both the liberal humanist fantasy of celebrating the diversity of queer identities and the empiricist fantasy to sample those identities representatively. With 'free-spirited' and 'batty boy' at play, the notion that we will one day add enough categories to 'lesbian, gay, bisexual, transgender, queer, questioning . . .' to saturate the possibility of representing identity categories seems as far off as the positivist fantasy of representing each category with a recognisable representative sample.

Experiments with normativity

Given these discursive limits of quantitative research, why would someone conduct social psychology experiments at all? My own work in this field exemplifies how the experimental study of situationism has changed since Milgram's time. Social psychologists are less regularly concerned with such big and dramatic demonstrations of the power of immediate situations as those constructed by Milgram or Zimbardo. In recent decades, as a result of ethical concerns raised by such experiments, and under the influence of cognitive psychology, we have become far more engaged with questions about how people make sense of their social worlds through attributions, stereotypes and cognitive heuristics (see Fiske and Taylor 1991).

As part of this shift, experimenters have often examined how and why people rigidly cling to beliefs in the face of evidence to the contrary. For example, in an early experiment Chapman and Chapman (1967) examined clinicians who erroneously judged that responses stereotypically associated with homosexuality were more likely to be produced in response to Rorschach cards by gay men than by others. Snyder and Uranowitz (1978) studied the ways that people selectively remembered events from a woman's life that are consistent with lesbian stereotypes after they learn that she has come out as lesbian. Deaux and Lewis (1984) showed that people described as transgressing norms for gender were more likely to be judged to be gay or lesbian than heterosexual. In other words, social psychology experiments have become ways of calling attention to the irrationality of modern life, and the impossibility of creating a social world in which people automatically reach consensus about what evidence means. Allport's (1954) positivist dream has been lost. My own experiments concerned the ways that people make sense of evidence about group differences by thinking normatively. The first experiments I carried out in this domain were concerned with the ways that heteronormativity affects the way that people explain differences between people categorised by sexual orientation. Felicia Pratto and I asked undergraduates to write explanations of scientific findings that we presented to them (see Hegarty and Pratto 2001, 2004). We told half of them that interview studies had shown that gay men and lesbians reported more gender non-conforming childhoods than heterosexual women and men. The other half was told that the heterosexuals recalled more gender non-conforming childhoods. The participants' written explanations were coded for references to members of each sexual orientation group. Participants overwhelmingly focused their explanations on behaviours, traits and other attributes of lesbians and gay men, but mentioned far fewer particularities of heterosexuals that might have contributed to the group differences. We were particularly concerned with *heteronormativity* in this research and, following Butler (1993), understood the new empirical research on gender-inversion models in psychology to normalise heterosexuality in at least three ways.

First, heterosexuals were taken as the norm for comparison, such that their particular attributes remained unspoken while those of lesbians and gay men incited psychological explanation. Second, the genders that are understood to be 'inverted' in this model are assumed to be heterosexuals' genders. The possibility that gay and lesbian genders might be the ontological basis for describing heterosexual genders beyond the epistemological horizon of gender-inversion theories, even though heterosexual genders might be most obviously performed through the disavowal of homosexuality. Third, in our experiments, the participants granted the evidence supporting gender-inversion models greater weight. These findings were essentialised and deemed to be reports of real childhood differences. In contrast, when we told participants that heterosexuals reported gender non-conforming experiences, they assumed that this meant that gay men and lesbians had lied to the interviewers or remembered their own childhoods wrongly. I will leave it to the reader to adjudicate whether this work is queer or not, but I have explained elsewhere how the experiments' design was informed by queer theory and the need to instantiate how people might think about group identities with non-essentialised categories (Barker and Hegarty 2005). The experiments were also conducted apropos of the resurgence of interest in gender-inversion models of homosexual development in psychology (e.g. Bailey and Zucker 1995; Bem 1996). We aimed to demonstrate that people make sense of such findings in culturally particular but systematic ways.

Similar findings have been observed when people explain other kinds of group differences; gender differences are explained by describing how women are different from men rather than how men are different from women (Miller, Taylor and Buck 1991). In the US, race differences are explained by taking whites' behaviour as the norm and explaining how blacks' behaviour differ from it (Pratto, Hegarty and Korchmaros in press). Explanations of group differences involve drawing on existing knowledge about those groups; they require the citation of stereotypes, and as such are occasioned performances rather than literal truths. However, scientists' explanations are readily confused with facts, and when such explanations are heteronormative they become a site where heteronormativity is sedimented. I think that these experiments not only say something about the stereotypes of participants but also trouble the methods of professional social scientists as well. Typically social cognition research assumes scientists to be more rational than laypeople, describing the cognitions of the latter group as error-prone, naïve, biased or intuitive versions of the former (e.g. Kahneman, Slovic and Tverksy 1982). This is a norm my colleagues and I are keen to publicly break. So far we have three methods for doing so.

First, we study scientists' explanations of group differences in their published texts as well as conducting experiments on undergraduates. Thus far, we have found that psychologists' and biologists' accounts of sexual orientation differences are routinely heteronormative (e.g. Hegarty 2003; Hegarty and Pratto 2001) and their accounts of gender differences are routinely androcentric (Hegarty and Buechel 2006). Second, we try to model what opposition to normativity would look like in the way that we describe our own results. In our experiments, people wrote sentences that compared gay people to straight people more than the reverse and preferred 'more than' constructions of difference to 'less than' constructions. In contrast, we pepper our results sections with sentences such as this one, 'Across the experiment as a whole, fewer references to straight men ($M =$ 0.49) than to gay men ($M = 0.78$) were produced, $F(1, 122) = 6.20, p < .05$' (Hegarty and Pratto 2001:727).

Some readers have told us that they have noticed this practice, suggesting that, as they read our experimental findings, their tacit knowledge about norms for explanations of group differences are also engaged by our writing practice. Like Lorde (1984), we understand such mythical norms as whiteness, Christianity, heterosexuality, etc. to inhabit the edge of consciousness; we *can* bring them into view but we habitually do not. Third, we openly describe ourselves as scientists situated within culture, whose thinking is shaped by the tacit knowledge we describe (see Hegarty and Pratto 2004:452). Thus, we work against the image of laypeople as a biased version of scientific rationality, concluding instead that 'psychologists are very ordinary, very much influenced by culture, and very much like other people' (Hegarty and Buechel 2006).

Conclusion

In this chapter I have argued that queering methodologies in psychology involves memory work, epistemological bravado, and literary subversion that cares enough about the ritualised practices of 'methodology' to blaspheme against them. The equation of critical work with qualitative work on psychology has opened up many new ways of producing knowledge about queerness, many of which are described in other chapters in this book. However, queer theory could be quantophilic as well as quantophobic. There is much to play for in laboratories, even if the play has been largely heteronormative for historical reasons (Lubek and Stam 1995). Access to experimental spaces where 'the social' is materialised through practices of artifice, performance and social roles has presented, and continues to present, difficulties for queers, who were deliberately excluded at its foundational moments. This is a space to which we must lay claim.

Notes

1 The 'GI Bill' or 1944 Serviceman's Readjustment Act provided college and vocational education for returning World War II veterans in addition to unemployment benefits and housing loans.

2 The *DSM* is the *Diagnostic and Statistical Manual*, the codification of psychiatric disorders institutionalised by the American Psychiatric Association. Both the first SM (published in 1952) and *DSM II* (published in 1968) listed homosexuality as a mental illness. Subsequent to the Association's vote to remove homosexuality in 1973, *DSM III* (published in 1980) listed only 'ego-dystonic homosexuality' to refer to lesbian and gay persons who themselves perceived their homosexuality to be an impediment to psychological adjustment. This category was removed from the revision to *DSM III* (published in 1987).

3 Paragraph 175 had banned 'unnatural fornication' among men in Germany since 1872. In 1935, under the Nazis, sodomy was categorised as a felony subject to a punishment of five years in prison, and arrests increased dramatically.

4 As one mental health nurse recalled it, 'We had to become electrifying geniuses! The situation was you had the screen, the person sat at the table with the things [equipment] on and with a lever that they had to pull to avoid the shocks. The pictures started off with pretty men, working their way through ugly men into ugly women and into pretty women. That was the whole process literally' (cited in Bartlett, King and Smith 2004:3).

5 In Zimbardo's experiment, male college student volunteers were randomly assigned to play the roles of 'prisoner' and 'guard' in a mock prison in the basement of Stanford's Psychology Department. Although the experiment was scheduled to run for two weeks, it was stopped after six days for ethical reasons. Accounts of this experiment attributed the guards' brutal behaviour and the prisoners' acquiescence to their roles in terms of the 'power of the situation' over the personality of the individual. While Zimbardo (1999) also reproduces this narrative, it also shows clearly that prisoners often rebelled individually and collectively and that guards' brutality was supported by Zimbardo's own dual role as 'experimenter' (outside the experiment) and chief prison guard (within it). My point here is that SM, at least as described by Townsend (2000) – who was exiting

a career in psychology around the same time that Zimbardo's experiment was garnering him fame within the discipline – had lessons for the ethical means of managing consent in situations where role-play and power are concerned; lessons which many within the discipline of social psychology were resistant to learning.

6 Here, it is worth remembering that the term 'subject' long used for participants in psychology experiments is derived from French pathologists' term for a corpse, see Danziger (1990).

7 In 1994 Sigma Research evolved from Project Sigma, which had conducted longitudinal research on the health of gay and bisexual men in the UK since 1987. SIGMA Research is 'a social research group specialising in the behavioural and policy aspects of HIV and sexual health' (www.sigmaresearch.org.uk/index.html).

References

Allport, G.W. (1954) The historical background of modern social psychology. In G. Lindzey (ed.), *Handbook of Social Psychology*. Worchester, MA: Clark University Press, pp. 1–50.

American Psychological Association (1994) *Publication Manual of the American Psychological Association*, 5th edn. Washington: American Psychological Association.

Aronson, E., Wilson, T.D. and Brewer, M.B. (1998) Experimentation in social psychology. In D.T. Gilbert, S.T. Fiske and G. Lindzey (eds), *Handbook of Social Psychology*. Boston: McGraw-Hill, pp. 99–142.

Bailey, J.M. and Zucker, K.J. (1995) Childhood sex-typed behaviour and sexual orientation: a conceptual analysis and quantitative review. *Developmental Psychology*, **31**, 43–55.

Barker, M. and Hegarty, P. (2005) Queer politics: queer science. *Psychology of Women Section Review*, **7**, 71–9.

Bartlett, A., King, M. and Smith, G. (2004) Treatment of homosexuality in Britain since the 1950s – an oral history: the experience of professionals. *British Medical Journal*, **328**, 427. BMJ, doi: 10.1136/bmj.37984.496725.EE

Bauman, Z. (1989) *Modernity and the Holocaust*. Cambridge: Polity Press.

Baumrind, D. (1964) Some thoughts on ethics of research: after reading Milgram's 'behavioral study of obedience'. *American Psychologist*, **19**, 421–3.

Bayer, R. (1981) *Homosexuality and American Psychiatry*. Princeton: Princeton University Press.

Bem, D.J. (1996) Exotic becomes erotic: a developmental theory of sexual orientation. *Psychological Review*, **103**, 320–35.

Bem, S.L. (1998) *An Unconventional Family*. New Haven: Yale Univeristy Press.

Bernal, J.D. (1965) *Science in History Volume 2: The Scientific and Industrial Revolutions*. Cambridge: MIT Press.

Berube, A. (1990) *Coming out Under Fire: The History of Gay Men and Women in World War Two*. New York: Macmillan.

Brown, R. (1986) *Social Psychology: The Second Edition*. New York: The Free Press.

Brown, R. (1989) Roger Brown. In G. Lindzay (ed.), *A History of Psychology in Autobiography*, volume 8. Stanford: Stanford University Press, pp. 37–60.

Butler, J. (1993) *Bodies That Matter*. New York: Routledge.

Capshew, J. (1999) *Psychologists on the March: Science, Practice and Professional Identity in America, 1929–1969*. Cambridge: Cambridge University Press.

Chapman, J.L. and Chapman, J.P. (1967) Genesis of popular but erroneous psychodiagnostic observations. *Journal of Abnormal Psychology*, **74**, 396–400.

Cherry, F. (1995) *The 'Stubborn Particulars' of Social Psychology: Essays on the Research Process*. London: Routledge.

Coyle, A. (2000) Qualitative research and lesbian and gay psychology in Britain. *Newsletter of the British Psychological Society Lesbian and Gay Section*, **4**, 2–5.

Danziger, K. (1990) *Constructing the Subject: Historical Origins of Psychological Research*. Cambridge: Cambridge University Press.

Darley, J. (1952) Contract support in psychology. *American Psychologist*, **7**, 719–21.

Deaux, K. and Lewis, L.L. (1984) Structure of gender stereotypes: interrelationships among components and gender label. *Journal of Personality and Social Psychology*, **46**, 991–1004.

Fiske, S.T. and Taylor, S.E. (1991) *Social Cognition*, 2nd edition. New York: McGraw-Hill.

Freedman, E.B. (1987) 'Uncontrolled desires': the response to the sexual psychopath, 1920–1960. *Journal of American History*, **74**, 830–106.

Gathorne-Hardy, J. (1998) *Sex: The Measure of All Things*. Bloomington: Indiana University Press.

Gentile, P. and Kinsman, G. (2000) Psychology, national security and the 'fruit machine'. *History and Philosophy of Psychology Bulletin*, **12**, 18–24.

Hegarty, P. (2001) 'Real science', deception experiments and the gender of my labcoat: toward a new laboratory manual for lesbian and gay psychology. *International Journal of Critical Psychology*, **1**, 91–108.

Hegarty, P. (2003) Pointing to a crisis: What finger-length ratios tell us about the construction of sexuality. *Radical Statistics*, **83**, 16–30.

Hegarty, P. and Buechel, C. (2006) Androcentric reporting of gender differences in APA articles, 1965–2004. *Review of General Psychology*, **10**, 377–389.

Hegarty, P. and Pratto, F. (2001) The effects of category norms and stereotypes on explanations of intergroup differences. *Journal of Personality and Social Psychology*, **80**, 723–35.

Hegarty, P. and Pratto, F. (2004) The differences that norms make: empiricism,social constructionism and the interpretation of group differences. *Sex Roles*, **50**, 445–53.

Herek, G.M. (1998) Bad science in the service of stigma: a critique of the Cameron group's survey results. In G.M. Herek (ed.), *Stigma and Sexual Orientation: Understanding Prejudice against Lesbians, Gay Men, and Bisexuals*. Thousand Oaks: Sage, pp. 223–55.

Herman, E. (1995) *The Romance of American Psychology: Political Culture in the Age of Experts*. Berkeley: University of California Press.

Hogg, M.A. and Vaughn, G.M. (2005) *Social Psychology*, 5th edition. Harlow: Prentice Hall.

Hooker, E. (1993) Reflections of a 40-year exploration: a scientific view on homosexuality. *American Psychologist*, **48**, 450–3.

Jones, J. (1997) *Alfred Kinsey: A Public/Private Life*. New York: Norton.

Kahneman, D., Slovic, P. and Tversky, A. (eds) (1982) *Judgment under Uncertainty: Heuristics and Biases*. Cambridge: Cambridge University Press.

Katz, J.N. (1976) *Gay American History: Lesbians and Gay Men in the U.S.A.* New York: Avon.

Kitzinger, C. (1997) Lesbian and gay psychology: a critical analysis. In D. Fox and I. Prilleltensky (eds), *Critical Psychology: An Introduction.* London: Sage, pp. 202–16.

Kitzinger, C. and Coyle, A. (2002) Introducing lesbian and gay psychology. In A. Coyle and C. Kitzinger (eds), *Lesbian and Gay Psychology: New Perspectives.* Oxford: Blackwell, pp. 1–29.

Linden, R.R. (1982) Introduction: against sadomasochism. In R.R. Linden, D.R. Pagano, D.E.H. Russell and S.L. Star (eds), *Against Sadomasochism: A Radical Feminist Analysis.* San Francisco: Frog in the Well, pp. 1–15.

Lorde, A. (1984) *Sister Outsider.* Crossing Press: Freedom, CA.

Lubek, I. and Stam, H.J. (1995) Ludicro-experimentation in social psychology: soberscientific versus playful prescriptions. *Trends and Issues in Theoretical Psychology.* Springer: New York, pp. 171–80.

Lutz, C. (1997) The psychological ethic and the spirit of containment. *Public Culture,* **9**, 135–59.

Marcus, E. (1992) *Making History: The Struggle for Gay and Lesbian Equal Rights, an Oral History.* New York: Harper Collins.

Milgram, S. (1974) *Obedience to Authority.* New York: Harper & Row.

Miller, D.T., Taylor, B. and Buck, M.L. (1991) Gender gaps: who needs to be explained? *Journal of Personality and Social Psychology,* **61**, 5–12.

Miller, N. (2002) *Sex-Crime Panic: A Journey to the Paranoid Heart of the 1950s.* Los Angeles: Alyson Books.

Minton, H.L. (1997) Queer theory: historical roots and implications for psychology. *Theory and Psychology,* **7**, 337–53.

Moore, A.M. (2005) Visions of sadomasochism as a Nazi erotic. *Lesbian & Gay Psychology Review,* **6**, 163–76.

Oliansky, A. (1991) A conferederate's perspective on deception. *Ethics & Behavior,* **1**, 253–8.

Orne, M.T. (1962) On the social psychology of the psychological experiment: with particular reference to demand characteristics and their implications. *American Psychologist,* **17**, 776–83.

Parlee, M.B. (1996) Situated knowledges of personal embodiment: transgender activists' and psychological theorists' perspectives on 'sex' and 'gender'. *Theory and Psychology,* **6**, 625–45.

Pratto, F., Hegarty, P. and Korchmairos, J. (in press) Who gets stereotyped? How communication practices and category norms lead people to stereotype particular people and groups. In Y. Kashima, K. Fiedler and P. Freytag (eds), *Stereotype Dynamics: Language-Based Approaches to Stereotype Formation, Maintenance, and Change.* Mahwah, NJ: Lawrence Erlbaum Associates.

Rubin, G.S. (1984) Thinking sex: notes for a radical theory of the politics of sexuality. In C.S. Vance (ed.), *Pleasure and Danger: Exploring Female Sexuality.* Boston: Routledge & Kegan Paul, pp. 157–210.

Sieber, J.E., Iannuzzo, R. and Rodriguez, B. (1995) Deception methods in psychology: have they changed in 25 years? *Ethics & Behavior,* **5**, 67–85.

Sisson, K. (2005) The cultural formation of S/M: history and analysis. *Lesbian and Gay Psychology Review,* **6**, 147–62.

Snyder, M. and Uranowitz, S.W. (1978) Reconstructing the past: some cognitive consequences of person perception. *Journal of Personality and Social Psychology*, **36**, 941–50.

Terry, J. (1999) *An American Obsession*. Chicago: University of Chicago Press.

Townsend, L. (2000) *The Leatherman's Handbook: Silver Jubilee Edition*. Beverley Hills: L.T. Publications.

Traweek, S. (1988) *Beamtimes and Lifetimes: The World of High Energy Physics*. Cambridge: Harvard University Press.

Walsh-Bowers, R. (1999) Fundamentalism in psychological science: the Publication Manual as 'bible'. *Psychology of Women Quarterly*, **23**, 375–92.

Warner, N. (2004) Towards a queer research methodology. *Qualitative Psychology*, **1**, 321–37.

Weatherburn, P., Reld, D., Hickson, F., Hammond, G. and Stephens, M. (2005) *Risk and Reflexion: Findings from the United Kingdom Gay Men's Sex Survey 2004*. London: Sigma Research.

Zimbardo, P.G. (1999) *The Quiet Rage: The Stanford Prison Study* [video]. New York: Insight media.

Glossary of terms

Aftercare the period after a BDSM scene when the top looks after the bottom, bringing them up from any submissive headspace and often praising them in general and in relation to the scene they have endured. For some this is almost more important than the scene itself.

Asexual not sexually attracted to others.

BDSM broad term for 'bondage and discipline, domination and sub-mission, and sadomasochism'. It encompasses all sexual identities and practices involving pain play, tying people up, taking dominant and submissive roles, and the erotic exchange of power.

Bisensual attracted to both genders, but not sexually.

Bisexual attracted to both genders and sexualities. Bisexuality may also be considered as transcending categories and is understood as a term that represents multiple perspectives and is therefore more than simply an identity.

Bondage restraining/restricting someone, e.g. with ropes, chains, cuffs.

Bottom slang term for a submissive/masochist, but generally meaning a person who enjoys being given various physical sensations as opposed to a 'submissive' who enjoys being controlled psychologically.

Cbt cock and ball torture – strong sensations to the male genitals.

Deconstruction a method of analysis that stems from the work of Derrida concerned with investigating the fundamentals of Western thought. It has become understood more broadly to be any method that seeks to critically examine the discursive foundations of our understandings.

Discipline training someone to behave in a certain way through punishment.

Dominant (dom/domme/dominatrix/master/mistress) person who takes control over others, e.g. giving orders, binding or 'torturing' them.

Ethical the term 'ethical' is used here in reference to Foucault's later work on sexuality where he separates a space of ethics (which relate to the self's relation to itself) from the notion of moral codes and identifies the various techniques through which we work (and are enjoined to work) upon ourselves in order to turn ourselves into ethical beings (that is within beings operating within a moral framework of some kind).

Gender identity   identity as a man or woman, i.e. two genders are used to represent individuals.

Genderqueer   not identifying with any particular gender.

Head space   state of mind somebody goes into during BDSM play (e.g. submissive/dominant headspace). Not all BDSMers talk in these terms.

Hermeneutics   methods of interpretation. These can be distinguished between those based on suspicion (using a specific framework of interpretation such as psychoanalysis) and those based on empathy (where one seeks to understand the phenomenon as it appears phenomenologically).

Heteropatriarchy   this is a condensation of the term 'heteronormativity' which can be defined as a complex of values, morals and ideals, operating at individual, institutional, social and cultural levels, which place heterosexuality (especially monogamous marriage) at the centre of understandings of love and sexuality, and where sexualities that fall outside these norms are devalued or pathologised in some way, and 'patriarchy' which refers to the dominant social and structural power and authority of men and masculinity.

Heterosexism   the widespread assumption of heterosexuality.

Hodological map   an idea from Sartre which he developed in his attempt to theorise human emotional life. It refers to the mental map of the paths which we believe we will follow to reach our goals, and through which we see the world before us as if it were of our own making.

Homonegativity   negative thoughts and feelings towards same-sex sexualities.

Identity   within psychology identity is often located within the individual, at the core of the person. Within sociology, identity is linked to the idea of 'self'. It is socially organised and dependent upon the interaction of the personal (or 'I') and social ('Me').

Kinky   general term for BDSM, fetish or non-vanilla sexual behaviour or people engaging in this.

Lifeworld   a term from the work of the philosopher Husserl (the founder of phenomenology) used to describe the world as concretely lived, as experienced (the foundation for all phenomenological research).

Modernity   marked the shift from traditional, pre-industrial societies to industrialisation and the sweeping changes in society during the nineteenth century across Europe. New forms of social organisation appeared, especially in relation to capital and labour. One major fact about modern societies rests with the idea that we rely on people we hardly know more and more. This is particularly relevant to the rise of therapy and the role of therapist as 'expert'. Some argue that this is still in place and that rather than entering postmodernity we are, in fact, in a period of late modernity.

Omnisexual attracted to all genders.

Pansexual attracted to all genders, sexes and sexualities.

Phenomenology the branch of philosophy founded by Husserl concerned with describing 'the things themselves'.

Play engaging in BDSM, e.g. 'I played with her', 'want to play?', or a specific activity e.g. nipple play, sensory deprivation play.

Postmodern contests the idea that certain foundational 'truths' exist and declares that all meta-narratives should come under scrutiny. This suggests, for example, that foundational categories such as 'man' and 'woman', 'heterosexual' and 'homosexual' should be deconstructed as their relevance exists in language and text, rather than in a certain 'truthfulness'. Some argue we are still in a stage of late modernity rather than postmodernity.

Queer theory hard to define but is concerned with disrupting binary categories of identity and therefore providing a radical challenge to many of the assumptions underpinning common-sense understandings of self and identity, in the West at least. It is a critical theoretical perspective particularly associated with the work of Judith Butler which challenges the notion of a unified homosexual (or indeed heterosexual).

Safeword a word that players can use to end the scene if it stops working for them.

Scene a BDSM encounter/session, sometimes divided into heavier/lighter scenes depending on physical and/or psychological intensity, although what constitutes this differs between people/occasions.

Sensation play term often used to describe play that involves physical stimulation, which may be pleasurable, painful or both.

Sex sex can refer to either sexual behaviour i.e. sexual acts, or to the biological differences between the two sexes of male and female i.e. the genital differences. Within some psychosocial accounts e.g. sociological accounts, the notion of 'sex' as only being male or female is challenged, and the suggestion that such a binary limits our understanding of the body has challenged the prevailing binarism.

Sexuality may be referred to as 'sexual orientation' or 'sexual identity'. There are problems with these terms as the former has taken on biological assumptions while the latter has come under scrutiny from those who contest the notion of a 'fixed' identity (e.g. Judith Butler), suggesting sexuality is fluid and changeable. Sexuality refers to our choice (the notion of 'choice' may also be questioned) of sexual partner and the labels heterosexual, homosexual, lesbian, intersexual, trans-sexual, bisexual etc. all refer to categories of sexual identity which are presently contested terms.

Subjectification   Foucauldian concept which refers to the processes through which subjectivities are created via the operation of power, the ways in which individuals are 'subjugated' via techniques and practices which enable the assembling of selves.

Submissive (sub/slave)   person who gives control over to others, e.g. obeying orders, being bound and/or 'tortured'.

Switch   person who can enjoy both sub/dom or top/bottom roles.

Top   slang term for dominant/sadist, but generally meaning a person who inflicts various physical sensations as opposed to a 'dominant' who enjoys being in control psychologically.

Torture   administered erotic pain.

Toys   devices designed for BDSM or sex (e.g. riding crops, paddles, nipple clamps, dildos) or used for this purpose (e.g. hairbrush, candle, clothes pegs).

Transmen (or FtMs)   individuals who were assigned the female gender at birth but identify as male.

Transpeople   individuals whose gender identity does not match that assigned at birth.

Transsexual   transpeople who identify unambiguously as either male or female and often desire medical treatment.

Transwomen (or MtFs)   individuals who were assigned the male gender at birth but identify as female.

Vaginoplasty   construction of an artificial vagina.

Vanilla   term sometimes used to describe non-BDSM, non-kinky sex. Also used to describe non-penetrative sex.

Appendix

A possible scenario from the perspective of a dominant

I sit on the edge of the bed. You kneel at my feet. Slowly, carefully, you unlace my boots. You slide my foot tenderly out of its shoe, then do the same for the other one. You peel the socks from my hot skin, tracing your fingers softly down my ankle, along my sole. You hold one foot in your lap, massaging it, pinching each toe gently, rubbing the tiredness of the day away. I watch you as you work. You gaze into my eyes as you raise my other foot to kiss your way along the bridge and across the toes. Your eyes are heavy with desire to please. There'll be no need to beat you into submission tonight. You're already there pet. Your look says it all. You belong to me. You'd do absolutely anything to please me. I lean my head back and sigh contentedly.

A possible scenario from the perspective of a submissive

We'd agreed that she would send some texts during the day before our date, but I hadn't expected this much. It started relatively easily, she ordered me to furtively masturbate and pinch myself, but as the day wore on she started getting me to do mildly embarrassing things in public, although nobody would be aware of it but me. There's always a feeling of power associated with being topped, but this day it was amplified enormously. I think the most challenging thing she did was to tell me I was only going to be allowed to come if I replied to a text message within 20 seconds. I managed it in 14. Later she said that being at work, knowing that I was anxiously waiting for my phone to beep was highly distracting. She was glad she didn't have much work to do that day. I certainly never thought I'd get so turned on by text messages. I still have them in my phone.

A possible scenario involving sensation play

Three men arrive at a club already filled with anticipation of the evening to come. First they sit on the sofas for a while chatting with friends. After some time they separate off to check in with each other that they are both still happy with what they planned the evening before. Then they move through to the play room. The tops tie the bottom to a bar on the wall so his hands are fastened above his head and his feet to the floor, legs spread. First one top runs a pinwheel over the bottom's back and thighs which gives a prickling sensation to his skin. Then the other taps a light wooden cane across his buttocks, gradually increasing the pressure until the feeling becomes mildly painful but pleasurable. Several times they check in with the bottom to find out where he is on a scale of one to ten (with ten being the most intense, almost unbearable, level of pain). The bottom experiences an endorphin rush from the experience and is aware of feeling the most relaxed that he has been all week. After the scene they retire to the sofas and all hug for a while. Later on in the evening they reverse roles and move once again to the play room for a different scene.

Index

Aaronson, Ian 61
abuse 114; childhood 113; internalised 111; sexual 66
actors: social 5, 41, 48–9
addiction 114
adrenal hyperplasia 54
affirmation 23
Against Sadomasochism: A Radical Feminist Analysis 130
AIDS 8
Alexander, Tamara 66
alienation 17, 19; social 25
ambiguity: sexual 33
American Psychiatric Association 73, 108, 127
American Psychological Association 131
Analysis Terminable and Interminable 63
Anderson, Barbara 85
androcentrism 135
androgen insensitivity syndrome 54
anger 23–35
antisocial personality disorder 115
assigned gender: rejection of 56–7, *see also* gender, reassignment of

Bateson, Gregory 91
behaviour: 'desirable, healthy, normal' 5
behavioural therapy 46
belief system: heterosexual 48; incongruence with lived experience 32–3
Bem, Daryl 127
Bem, Sandra 127
Beyond the Pleasure Principle 64
binary categories 1–2, 42–3, 90; challenge to 3, 27, 48, 89; comfort of 6; and identity models 4, 38–9; and trans 76–7, 81, 84–5

biopolitics 20n4
birth certificates: alterations to 82
bisexuality 4, 26, 38; inherent 63; primal disposition to 59, 68n3; psychic 59
bondage/discipline, domination/ submission and sadomasochism (BDSM) 3, 5, 83; assumptions about 115–16; challenges and potentials of 106–24; dominant discourses of 112–16, 121n8; introduction to 107–9; legality of 108; motivations for 112, 121n7; negative client experiences 112–16; pathologisation of 108–9, 120–1n5; perceived threat of 106; as play 110; positive client experiences 116–19; prevalence of 107–8; promotional slogans for 111; and queer theory 109–12, 120–1n5; role play scenarios 145–6; sexual content of 114–15
bottoms 108, 113, 120n3
boyfriends 92–4
British Association for Counselling and Psychotherapy (BACP) 45
British Psychological Society (BPS) 46, 102
Brown, George 79
Brown, Roger 127
Butler, Judith 3, 8–12, 19, 20n3, 90, 131, 133–4

case studies: Alex and Lisa 81; Athena 96–7; Belinda, Jenny and Lee 80; Fatima and Abdul 95–6; Jack 57; Jason and Eve 81–2; Javier 32–3; Jonathan and Kai 92–4; Jose and Peter 98–9; Kristin 64–5; Louise 78–9; Lulu 37–8, 49; Marielle 58–9;